Minority Peoples

In the Age of Nation-States

African Diaspora Research Project
Urban Affairs Programs
Michigan State University
East Lansing, MI 48824 -- USA

D0920352

Minority Peoples
In the Age of Nation-States

EDITED BY GÉRARD CHALIAND
TRANSLATED BY TONY BERRETT
FOREWORD BY BEN WHITAKER

Pluto **A** Press

GROUPEMENT POUR LES DROITS DES MINORITÉS

First published 1989 by Pluto Press
11–21 Northdown Street, London N1 9BN

Copyright © Gérard Chaliand 1989
Translation copyright © Pluto Press 1989

Printed and bound in the United Kingdom by
Billing & Sons, Worcester

All rights reserved

**British Library Cataloguing in Publication
Data**

Minority peoples in the age of nation-states
   1.   Social minorities
   I.   Chaliand, Gérard. *1934* -   II. Berrett,
Michael
   305

ISBN 0–7453–0276–9
ISBN 0–7453–0286–6 pbk

Contents

Foreword

BEN WHITAKER

The Minority Rights Group was started in the late 1960s at the time of the Biafran war in Nigeria. A number of concerned academics, intellectuals and journalists, including David Astor (the then editor-owner of the *Observer*), met in London to decide what best might be done; their conclusion was that once inter-communal hostility becomes so polarized that it erupts into violence — whether in Nigeria or Northern Ireland — the time is too late. The task of trying to further multi-cultural understanding, if not toleration, must start much earlier if violence — in which the innocent are most often the victims — is to be averted.

Hence the genesis of MRG, whose three principal aims are remedial, preventive and educational:

- To secure justice for minority (or majority) groups suffering discrimination by investigating their situation and publicising the facts as widely as possible to educate and alert public opinion throughout the world.
- To help prevent, through publicity about violations of human rights, such problems from developing into dangerous and destructive conflicts which, when polarized, are very difficult to resolve.
- To foster, by its research findings, international understanding of the factors which create prejudiced treatment and group tensions, thus helping to promote the growth of a world conscience regarding human rights.

The words 'or majority' were added in reference to groups meriting concern because MRG interprets 'minority' in terms of lack of power and status, not merely numerically: it has published reports on Blacks in Namibia, for example, and on women in Arab countries.

MRG commissions reports as resources permit; these are decided on criteria of urgency and with due regard to political and geographical balance. Another important role for MRG is to help provide a voice for oppressed minorities at the UN Human Rights sessions. Two years ago it succeeded in putting the massive tragedy of female circumcision on the UN agenda for the first time. As much as possible, we help members of minorities themselves to speak as witnesses in international meetings. Part of our work, in my view, is to try to articulate especially the problems and viewpoints of usually silent victims, such as migrant workers and exploited children.

The task of changing world opinion is a long-term one. Amnesty International, with which MRG regularly cooperates on a friendly basis (the simplest way to explain MRG is that it tries to do for groups worldwide what Amnesty does for individuals), has in some ways an easier role: people more readily identify sympathetically with an individual political victim than with, say, the Gypsies or the Kurds. But there are now MRG groups supported by volunteers in 16 different countries throughout the world — the most recent additions being in India, Austria, Denmark and Kenya. The French group (GDM, 19 rue Jacob, 75006 Paris), one of the strongest and earliest to be formed, has produced valuable reports on its own on *Les Kurdes en Iran*, *Les Corses*, and *Les Autochtones du Vietnam*. In 1982 MRG was awarded the United Nations Association's Media Peace Prize. Last year, 37,352 copies of MRG's reports were sold in 135 different countries (an increase of 13,227 over the year before) in addition to copies which are regularly sent free to journalists and others throughout the world. But much more remains to be done both in terms of work (there are over 40 more reports MRG would like to commission if it had the funds), and in terms of readership and supporters.

Was Gandhi right when he stated that civilization should be judged by its treatment of minorities? Today, a great number of large or small groups of people are suffering discrimination — sometimes even in cases where they form the majority in a society. Many of these problems are residual legacies of colonialism, with its arbitrary boundaries, importation of labour or the historic technique of dividing-and-ruling by playing off one race or tribe against another. And anti-semitism, apartheid, and Northern Ireland's 'double-minority' reminds us that such wholesale violations of human rights are just as capable of occurring in allegedly developed countries. Tensions from such situations are now on the increase as more and more groups (not excluding women) are unwilling to continue playing the role of victims — either of oppression or of pity.

Perhaps there is no such thing as a minority problem — only the problems of majority attitudes. In an address in Boston in 1860, Wendell Phillips said: 'Governments exist to protect the rights of minorities. The loved and the rich need no protection — they have many friends and few enemies.' Dr Conor Cruise O'Brien has argued that it is wrong to speak of minority rights or majority rights. 'Rights are best thought of as inherent in each human being, irrespective of what kind of cultural grouping he or she may belong to,' he said in his 1972 Minority Rights Group lecture.

> **The culture of a group may include** systematic violations of basic human rights. When we are told to respect the cultures of groups we are **being** told to respect things which may include for example the Hindu caste system, the treatment of women in Islam and a number of other cultures.... The Universal Declaration of Human Rights always prefers to speak of rights inherent in individual human beings and not of group rights.

The Minority Rights Group operates on the theory that alerted world opinion is the only real safeguard for human rights. However idealistically one may draft international charters or laws, in the long term their effectiveness depends on the active, informed concern of the public and the press to see that they are implemented. The first crime of Northern Ireland was that it was not until the violence began that people outside paid any attention to the discrimination there. It is encouraging that — as Amnesty International has found — even some recalcitrant dictatorships show themselves sensitive to criticism, prompted perhaps by the spread of television, international finance and tourism. The majority of governments recognize that their standing in the world cannot be allowed to deteriorate too far. Opinion outside their frontiers can in some cases be more important to them than domestic reactions. But ironically the oppression by a majority in a democracy can be a more intractable problem than persecution by a tyrant — at least the death of the latter can hold out a hope of relief. The predicament of poor people, when they form an economic minority in an affluent country, illustrates this problem.

On the other hand, it does no service, least of all for minorities, to idealize them. Some minorities are far from faultless (liberals tend to forget that people do not become virtuous merely by reason of their suffering); and of course majorities too have their rights as well as their responsibilities. One of the most interesting questions raised by group stigmatization is why some minorities are seen as a threat or a scapegoat while others are tolerated. Psychologists at Bristol University have found evidence that as soon as people are divided into groups — teams, clubs, unions, nations — they automatically begin to discriminate against non-member outsiders. Many species besides humans fear and attack nonconformity; indeed it has been argued that all people need a pecking-order and a group to look down upon — until in turn they are united by a new enemy. Perhaps it is in order to avoid facing up to the less pleasant parts of ourselves, or through failure to realize the real roots of our frustrations, that we project our aggression and fear on to other safer targets — of whom visibly distinct groups such as immigrants, women or policemen are often the most easily available.

Prejudice is often greatest among those who have least experience of immigrants or minorities, and have their own interests least affected by them. But prejudice can also be insidious and subtle. It can come in many forms: especially to those who think themselves immune to it. Here prejudice can be disguised as paternalism or even sympathy. 'We have met the enemy, and it is us,' as Walt Kelly said. At times one may think our generation beyond hope, and that we should concentrate our efforts on our successors. Psychologists suggest that a tolerant attitude is encouraged by the security of a person's early upbringing together with an education that tries to give people insight into their own weaknesses.

MRG has recently embarked on a major educational campaign which includes a slide-tape show, video and exhibition about minorities, and has employed an experienced teacher to visit schools in London to help develop awareness of racial and sexist prejudices. It has also organized prize competitions about human rights and posters about equal opportunity to widen the concerned constituency, especially among young people.

Each of us as an individual, of course, is a minority. The really unforgivable inhumanity is our habit of viewing a person not as him or herself, but distorted by a group judgement generated by often tribal or irrational emotions. As a defence against the complexities of life, we all categorize people, generally on very inadequate evidence. Few are the communicators in any country who do not at least unconsciously glorify their own race, sex and nationality. Ethnocentrism — the belief in the extraordinary value of one's own group, coupled with a suspicion of anything different — permeates homes, schools, books and newspapers throughout the world. (Note, for instance, how Asians or black Africans arriving to live in Europe are called 'immigrants' or worse — whereas Europeans living in their countries are called 'settlers'.) Rare indeed is the history book which is not riddled with implicit ethnocentric and nationalistic value-judgements. An international and impartial series of new history books that does not, for example, treat Africa principally through the eyes of white people is badly needed.

Prejudices are used as pretexts for denigrating political, social or economic opponents and provide us with excuses to exploit other classes, races or women. Leaders use them as calculated weapons; the led, driven by their need for security, shelter behind such blinkers and thereby are diverted from focusing upon the real causes of the injustices they are suffering. But this is not the result of any contemporary demagogue's new trick. Long before Hitler, political manipulators were seeking to bid for popularity by channelling public emotion on to vulnerable scapegoats, and thus cynically distracting society from the harder reality of confronting social or economic inequality. Minorities often appear to reveal wider social problems and come to be identified with them. Much inter-ethnic conflict is due not to pluralism but to societies' imbalances of power. Prejudice, which is also capable of being self-fulfilling, can be reinforced by competition in jobs, sex or housing. Gandhi's dictum about the treatment of minorities is thus a penetrating insight into the true nature of injustice.

In the opposite direction, several minority groups have shown a recent resurgence of interest in ideas of autonomy, perhaps as part of a wish to decentralize society (increasingly felt to be anonymously alien with the development of huge bodies such as the EEC) and break down its impersonality. Ralf Dahrendorf has argued: 'For freedom in society means, above all, that we recognize the justice and creativity of diversity, difference, and conflict.' In some parts of the United States, new ethnicity programmes are attempting to educate children to accept and respect their own rights and to learn that others' differences do not imply inferiority. Previously, many immigrants had been under pressure to shed their past and to be fused into an all-American identity — often a euphemism for white Anglo-Saxon Protestant values. Many but not all minority groups prefer mutual tolerance to synthesis in a society: integration — defined by Roy Jenkins as 'equal opportunity accompanied by cultural diversity in an atmosphere of tolerance' — is favoured over assimilation. (It is interesting that some of the Britons who complain loudest against immigrants' failure to become grey British stereotypes in the UK are those who would never have dreamed of adopting native customs, clothing, food or even language when they inhabited British possessions abroad.) I would suggest that the decision to integrate or assimilate should be one for the individual; but any such choice requires that both options are available. As Tagore states, 'The wideworld problem today is not how to unite with all differences, but how to unite with all differences intact... when natural differences find their harmony, then it is true unity.'

Each minority situation MRG studies has its distinct and unique components: historical, economic, psychological, sociological. But some useful common lessons may be found in the roots of prejudice, discrimination and stereotyping.

Above all, I believe we must urgently press for the establishment of a permanent impartial international Human Rights Tribunal, and also for an international ombudsman — preferably an effectively financed and staffed United Nations Commission for Human Rights — which could investigate and report on any oppression of groups or individuals. The essential need for non-governmental organizations such as MRG and Amnesty International arises because of the UN's failure to date to establish a strong human rights machinery. Almost every UN member government has several minorities or other groups suffering discrimination inside its borders and a consequent interest in blocking a human rights commission. This is not to underestimate the difficulties. (Secession, in particular, is a thorny problem. Mindful of the trouble of the previous League of Nations' Minorities Commission, the authors of the 1960 UN Declaration on Colonial Independence produced a classic example of ambiguity which asserted both the right of all peoples to self-determination and the right of all countries to freedom from any attempt to disrupt their national unity and territorial integrity.) But at present the UN lacks any effective procedure for safeguarding even the minimal rights of people in member states, unless and until their problems become a threat to international peace — a proviso that puts an unnecessary premium on violence. Nevertheless we should remember that the UN charter begins with the words, 'We, the peoples....' not 'We, the governments.' For who can know whether they in turn will not be an unpopular minority tomorrow?

Preface

GÉRARD CHALIAND

Minority Peoples in the Age of Nation-States is the first attempt to conceptualize the question of minority peoples in the late twentieth century. All nations of the world have their minority peoples, who frequently speak a different language, who live apart from the minority of the population, who dress differently and who have a different religion. The particular problems of such minority peoples have, until now, been largely overlooked. This book focuses on non-democratic societies as we define them in the West. In the West, minorities are *usually* able to make their voices heard without having to resort to violence. In the Third World, in the last 15 years, problems affecting a minority people — often expressed through violence as a last resort — appear more and more frequently on the agenda: Kurds in Iraq, Iran and Turkey; South Sudan; Tibet; Tamils in Sri Lanka; Eritreans; Sikhs, etc.

We have chosen not to discuss the problem of minorities in sub-Saharan Africa, where we have what are called nation-states but where in reality there are States and yet no Nations — in the sense that there is a Chinese, a Vietnamese or an Egyptian nation. The colonial division of borders, the multi-ethnic composition of nearly all states (except Somalia) means that everybody in sub-Saharan Africa belongs to a minority.

In Latin America, the Indian problem is important in five countries: Guatemala (where the so-called Indian minority is in fact a majority), Ecuador, Peru, Bolivia and, to a lesser extent, Mexico. The particularity of integration in the Spanish empire or in today's Latin American states is not racial but cultural: one is called a *mestizo* as soon as he or she speaks Spanish.

India, as is well known, is more a civilization than a nation. The very structure of its traditional society was a division by castes. In recent times, an attempt to create a more democratic society has had to suppress, at least officially, the caste system, and build a federation where most of the important linguistic and ethnic groups of the country have a state. The exclusion of some religious (such as the Sikhs) or ethnic (such as the Gurkhas) groups from that process has led to grievances and violence. Given the enormous diversity of minority groups, however, India appears, at least on the surface, to have coped rather well.

The logic of the content of this book has been to emphasize on the one hand the conceptual framework of minorities in the age of the nation-state and, on the other, to focus on two of the largest and probably the least well known civilizations of the Third World, China and Islam, representing together more than two billion people, and on a multi-ethnic or multi-racial empire, the Soviet Union. The second part of this book deals with three concepts: diaspora, genocide and ethnocide. A minority is not automatically a diaspora, although diasporas are always minorities. There are, in fact, very few diasporas. Born from a forced dispersion, they conscientiously strive to keep a memory of the past alive and foster the will to transmit a heritage and to survive as a diaspora. The classic example is the Jewish diaspora. We could add more recent examples, as time is an important factor: the Armenians, the Chinese in Southeast Asia, the Indians in the Indian Ocean, South Africa and the West Indies, and possibly, if the present situation continues, the Palestinians.

Genocide, a word coined by the jurist Lemkin after the Second World War, is the project put into execution by a sovereign state to exterminate an ethnic, religious or linguistic group (according to the definition of the United Nations, which excluded political groups, for instance). It has been applied in this century to the Armenians in 1915-16, the Jews and the Gypsies by the Nazis during the Second World War, etc. It is always a temptation for a non-democratic state (genocides are only organized by the state) either to terrorize or massively liquidate a minority. The logic of the far right in South Africa would be — if it were possible — to exterminate the Blacks rather than to surrender white political power.

Ethnocide is a word used to describe forced cultural integration usually among small groups of aborigines. Ethnocide usually precipitates the violent collapse of the group as such. Acculturation, as noted by the ethnologist F. Fonval, is a less painful route whereby a group gradually loses its identity consciously or unconsciously and is acculturated to other values imposed by a stronger group.

Minority Peoples
In the Age of Nation-States

GÉRARD CHALIAND

The 'problems' of minority peoples as we know them today are historically of very recent origin. Contemporary minority 'problems' stem directly from the nation-state; originally, in Europe, and even more recently in the East, minorities were perceived only as religious minorities.

The nation-state (which dates from the late eighteenth century) is a construct which we now take for granted as a 'natural' or eternal political state of affairs. But until the beginning of the modern industrial era, centralized authority had great difficulty in holding on to power and authority over long distances. Political boundaries tended to be fluid. It is only in recent times, with the rigid definitions of political boundaries and the advent of centralized government within those political boundaries, that 'minority peoples' have become the political 'problems' we know today.

Furthermore, it is not only that minority peoples have become problems within our modern nation-states, they have become problems which appear to be unresolvable. As a consequence minorities fight for ever smaller and smaller sized nation-states of their own to protect their human rights from the ravages, as they see it, of the wider nation-state or states in which they exist. The Kurds, the Protestant Irish, Tamils and Eritreans, to mention just a few examples, illustrate this simple point; everywhere minority peoples are fighting with their lives against great military odds.

The development of the nation-state in the late eighteenth century led to the gradual appearance in Europe during the nineteenth and early twentieth centuries of 'national minorities' based on ethnic or linguistic criteria. Until then, ethnic and/or linguistic peculiarities within a state had been seen as of minor importance. Obviously civilizations and societies over the centuries differed in their views of the problems of minorities,[1] but very often the factor of religious differentiation was fundamental.

The first manifestations of modern nationalism were the American Revolution in 1776 and the French Revolution of 1789. In a world that was everywhere except England based on the goodwill of the prince or despot, the American Declaration of Independence and the Universal Declaration of the Rights of Man were documents of an electrifying novelty.

> When in the Course of human events, it becomes necessary for one people to dissolve the political bands that have connected them with another, and to assume among the powers of the earth, the separate and equal station to which the Laws of Nature and of Nature's God entitle them, a decent respect to the opinions of mankind requires that they should declare the causes which impel them to the separation. We hold these truths to be self-evident, that all men are created equal, that they are endowed by their Creator with certain unalienable Rights, that among these are Life, Liberty and the pursuit of Happiness.

The Declaration of Independence proclaimed both the inalienable rights of man and the right of one people to throw off the political bonds that have attached it to another.

The Declaration of the Rights of Man and of the Citizen of 1789 spelled out this notion of the rights of man. For the French revolutionaries, the system of the rights of man was based on the principle of the sovereignty of a people; only a government resting on this principle, they wrote, made possible the full development of both individual rights and national sovereignty.[2]

The concept of the nation-state arose against the background of this new vision of the world. This model saw itself as democratic since it was based on the principle of the sovereignty of the people. But it had a built-in limitation: when nationalist ideology becomes aggressive, the result is the exclusion, rejection and even diabolization of the nationalism of others.

The nation-state as a single model gradually imposed itself on the rest of the world. Empires, whether Spanish or Portuguese in the Americas, Ottoman, Austro-Hungarian or, after the Second World War, colonial, gave way to states which sought to be nations.

The aspect of the nation-state model, based on democracy and con-sensus, that was generally imitated was not its potential for popular sover-eignty, but the building of the state — the nation being very often lacking, notably in heterogeneous sub-Saharan Africa.[3] A homogeneous population is an exception. The corollary of heterogeneity has been almost always — at least in the contemporary period — the absence of national consciousness.

The First World War and its aftermath put the right of (European) peoples to self-determination and the problem of nationalities back in the forefront. These ideas were expressed both by the American president

Woodrow Wilson and by Lenin. In fact, the right of peoples to self-determination figures in Woodrow Wilson's Fourteen Points as well as in the Declaration of the Rights of the Toiling Masses (Moscow, January 1918). Following the disappearance of the Hapsburg empire, the map of central Europe was redrawn as best as could be on the model of the nation-state (Poland, Czechoslovakia, Yugoslavia, etc.). Numerous minority problems remained, some of which were later the pretexts for, and some the victims of, the Second World War.[4] After the war, the United Nations Charter signed in June 1945 in San Francisco set out, explicitly this time, the rights of peoples and the rights of man. Article 55 of the Charter proclaims 'respect for the equal rights and self-determination of peoples' and 'universal respect for, and observance of, human rights and fundamental freedoms for all without distinction as to race, sex, language, or religion'.

The right of peoples to self-determination is mentioned twice in the United Nations Charter. It appears first in article 1, which sets out the purposes of the organization; paragraph 2 asserts that one of these aims is 'to develop friendly relations among nations based on respect for the principle of equal rights and self-determination of peoples, and to take other appropriate measures to strengthen universal peace'. It is mentioned again in article 55:

> With a view to the creation of conditions of stability and well-being which are necessary for peaceful and friendly relations among nations based on respect for the principle of equal rights and self-determination of peoples, the United Nations shall promote ...

On 10 December 1948, the United Nations General Assembly adopted the Universal Declaration of Human Rights which was completed by two international covenants adopted unanimously by the General Assembly in 1966: an International Covenant on Economic, Social, and Cultural Rights and an International Covenant on Civil and Political Rights. The first articles of the two human rights covenants read:

> 1. All peoples have the right to self-determination. By virtue of that right they freely determine their political status and freely pursue their economic, social and cultural development.
> 2. All peoples may, for their own ends, freely dispose of their natural wealth and resources without prejudice to any obligations arising out of international economic co-operation, based on the principle of mutual benefit, and international law. In no case may a people be deprived of its own means of subsistence.
> 3. The States Parties to the present Covenant, including those having

responsibility for the administration of Non-Self-Governing and Trust Territories, shall promote the realization of the right of self-determination, and shall respect that right, in conformity with the provisions of the Charter of the United Nations.

As J.-F. Guilhaudis very accurately points out, it is only at first glance that these articles appear to reproduce what was the core of the classical concept formulated at the time of the Enlightenment by the American and French Declarations.

As it moved from one continent to others,[5] the notion of self-determination encountered other concerns, other passions, and it became charged with new elements. The obsession with decolonization and the fragility of the new devotees of the idea of self-determination have shaped in a very original manner the right of peoples to secede and achieve independence. On the other hand, the search for a true, real freedom has taken the right of peoples already forming states into a new domain, the economic domain. Finally, by combining, these two passions have caused the old ambiguity of the principle of self-determination to disappear. They have given it an ideological unity and, by placing both among the demands of the struggle against colonialism, have blurred the distinction between two rights that are in fact very different: the right of peoples not forming a state to self-determination and the right of peoples already forming a state to self-determination.

In fact both the United Nations Organization (notably in article 1, paragraph 2 of the Charter) and international practice over recent decades have stressed not the right of peoples to form states but the right of self-determination to peoples already forming states. In reality, in the last forty years the right of peoples to self-determination has been, for the most part, the right of colonized peoples to free themselves from control by the West.[6]

Discussing minorities in the contemporary world amounts to examining one of the basic — and most complex — features of politics on the world scale.

Between the rights of man that protect the rights of individuals and the rights of states that regulate sovereignly everything falling within their 'domestic jurisdiction', minorities have virtually no effective rights recognized by international law. Their fate depends ultimately on the goodwill or degree of democracy of the state. It is stating the obvious to say that many minorities, especially in non-democratic states, suffer from discrimination and oppression without having any recourse, notably at the international level. In the forty years that it has existed, the International Court of Justice has not once been called upon to look into a minority problem. Nor has the European Court of Human Rights, since the European Convention on Human Rights and Fundamental Freedoms signed in Rome on 4 November 1950 contains no provisions regarding minorities.

The question of minorities in the contemporary world poses a double problem: on the one hand, regarding human rights, that of discrimination and oppression against them, as members of a group; on the other, at the level of states — and more particularly of the numerous new states that have not yet achieved their national integration — that of dissident movements and possible secession or destabilizing manipulation of ethnic factors by other states.[7]

In this book we deal with ethnic, religious and linguistic minorities — categories which may sometimes overlap.[8]

Since the virtual settlement of the colonial problem, minority questions have precipitated violent conflicts all over the world: Biafra (Nigeria); Eritrea and Tigre (Ethiopia); Baluchis (Pakistan); Kurds (Iraq and Iran); Tibet (China); Karens and Kachens (Burma); Mizos and Nagas (India); South Sudan; Lebanon; the Catholic minority in Northern Ireland; Tamils in Sri Lanka, etc.

In order to gain a clear idea of the great diversity of situations facing minorities in the world today, we need a few definitions and an attempt at a typology.

The minority phenomenon arises from a series of historical events. We cannot describe these events exhaustively, but two classic characteristics of the development of minority communities can be summarized:

• Historic minorities long settled in a given territory and surrounded by or partly interspersed with populations that have subsequently invaded these territories. Very often, these minorities find refuge in mountainous areas: the Caucasus, the Balkans, the Atlas in the Maghrib, Kurdistan, the mountains of Indochina, south-eastern China, the high Andes, etc. The Lebanese mountains represent an exemplary microcosm of a refuge-zone for religious minorities.

• Minority populations introduced by force into a new area such as the Blacks from Africa on the American continent or the Indians (from India) transplanted by the British as indentured labour to South Africa, the West Indies, etc.; or minorities who have left their country for religious, political or economic reasons and who have become, when they fail to assimilate, diaspora minorities (the Chinese in Southeast Asia, for example). In the latter case these are *non-territorial* minorities.

Minorities can become assimilated;[9] history is full of such cases. That implies the disappearance of collective memory. There is a loss of identity and dilution into the culture of the majority population. If they survive — and in this respect the main criterion is for how long — there is, with considerable variations in the degree of integration, conservation of a religious and/or cultural heritage. For many minorities, especially non-territorial ones, integration may be the stage which precedes a gradual assimilation.

Temporary or recent population movements cannot be included in a typology. These involve, on the one hand, movements in sub-Saharan Africa (which has the largest number of refugees),[10] the Middle East, Pakistan and Southeast Asia (in 1985 there were some 15 million refugees in the world) and, on the other, labour migration in North America and Western Europe, which has often changed from being temporary to being permanent.[11] How many of these groups will consider themselves to be minorities in 50 years' time in Africa, the Middle East or the West?

What is a minority? There is no simple answer to this question and it is tempting to limit the risks by replying that an ethnic, religious or linguistic minority is defined first of all by its own group consciousness in the long run. There is no minority without a collective memory. (The time dimension seems all the more important because history is full of groups that were minorities for varying lengths of time before blending into a larger whole, a phenomenon which there is no call to judge as necessarily negative.) However, since we are dealing with the problem of minorities in the age of the nation-state, we must essentially use, at this stage, the group's *collective will to survive*.[12]

Only groups that see themselves as different — ethnically, religiously or linguistically — and are concerned to preserve their special features, however integrated they may otherwise be as citizens of the state, should be described as minorities.

Demands relating to the status of minorities would be meaningless if they were dominant minorities. The White minority in South Africa is the obvious case, but it is not the only one. There is the classic example of the Tutsi in Burundi in Africa;[13] in Iraq there is the domination of the minority Sunni Arabs and, in Syria, even more striking, that of the Alawites — barely 15 per cent of the population.

Nor are we dealing with what Pierre George[14] calls 'superior minorities', those that demonstrate an attachment to a cultural heritage seen by the minority as superior to that of the majority population. This is particularly the case with the communities of German origin in Latin America; mainly in Argentina and Chile, but also in Peru, Bolivia and Guatemala.

We are dealing here, to adopt what I feel to be an adequate definition,[15] with a group of citizens of a state, numerically a minority and not dominant in this state, with ethnic, religious or linguistic characteristics different from those of the majority of the population, bound up with one another, animated, if only implicitly, by a collective will to survive and aiming at de facto and de jure equality with the majority.

This formulation is adequate for many countries — notably democratic ones — but to avoid two serious problems we need to add, on the one hand, that the special features of the minority must be recognized and can be perpetuated (which implies the right to identity and cultural rights),[16] and on the other hand, ask that their protection be ensured against possible physical excesses by the majority.[17]

In short, what is aimed at here regarding ethnic, religious or linguistic minorities are minorities that want to continue to exist and be recognized as such and, feeling themselves discriminated against or oppressed, want their protection assured and their rights recognized. These rights are of two sorts: equality *de jure* and *de facto* with the majority of the population of the state concerned whose citizens they are; and recognition by the state of their identity and the granting of cultural rights.

In fact, consciousness of belonging to a minority leads to recognition of the existence and specific features of that minority. It is accompanied by demands in the area of cultural rights: being able to use its language, learn it at school, publish freely, etc.

For territorial minorities (those that continue to occupy their territory), the major demand relates to the recognition of the specific character of the occupied territory. For extra-territorial minorities, the most common demand relates to securing all the rights enjoyed by the majority population and the right to maintain freely their particular features.

Non-dominant ethnic, religious or linguistic minorities are not defended here either as exemplary victims or because they are, by their essence, endowed with particular virtues. History is not exactly devoid of examples of victims becoming tyrants when circumstances allow. But they merit close attention because as a particularly vulnerable group they are frequently the object of discrimination or oppression, especially in non-democratic regimes.

Minorities, even those which are oppressed or suffering the sporadic violence of the majority group, are not necessarily the most disadvantaged group although this is frequently the case. A number of minorities that are particularly industrious and enterprising have been periodically (as was the case with the Jews in Eastern Europe) victims of the wrath, spontaneous or not, of majorities that are often less active; the attacks on the Chinese in Indonesia and the Tamils in Sri Lanka are but two instances.

In the contemporary world, the examples of minorities discriminated against or oppressed in varying degrees are so numerous that it is difficult even to compile a complete list of groups of any size. The problems they face are of all types:

- discrimination: rejection precipitated by membership of a particular group;
- cultural oppression: prohibition on studying one's own language in school or using it in publications or audiovisual materials;
- economic oppression: when the interests of the minority are systematically disadvantaged;
- physical oppression: massive settlement by the majority ethnic group or occupation of the territory of the minority by population transfer;
- genocide: a policy put into effect to eliminate the whole of a community.

It would seem that the minimum that should be guaranteed by an international jurisdiction — involving at least the moral condemnation by an international tribunal of states that do not enforce this minimum — should be the recognition of the specific features and of the cultural rights making it possible to maintain them. It goes without saying that a jurisdiction involving *de jure* and *de facto* equality will sooner or later be written into the framework of non-discrimination and the protection of minorities. But this will be meaningless unless an international court endowed with moral prestige can deliberate on the behaviour of this or that state. *It remains the case that ultimately the struggle for minorities is no more separate than the struggle for human rights from the struggle for democracy.*

The right to identity and cultural and religious rights should be declared inalienable. No state can deny anyone the right to be what he is, to practice his religion or to study and enrich his culture.

It is absolutely scandalous, for example, that Algeria should deny or attempt to deprive Berber-speakers of their linguistic and cultural identity. No argument based on considerations relating to the colonial period can justify the pretence of a solely Arab Algeria linguistically speaking.[18] The *de facto* banning of the Berber-speaking culture in Kabylia and the Aurès mountains particularly in favour of a centralized (and mythical) structure is precisely the least positive heritage of the colonial period. What can be said about the Kurds in Turkey where their very existence is denied? This case is unique in the contemporary world.

Among the hundreds and hundreds of minorities discriminated against, oppressed, forgotten or simply unknown, we cannot avoid mentioning the

Indian populations of Latin America,[19] grievously marginalized over the centuries and still strangers in their own countries: in Guatemala, Peru, Ecuador and Bolivia. We cannot avoid recalling, in the dying years of the Ottoman empire, the genocide of the Armenians, the liquidation of the Greeks in Asia Minor and the massacres of the Assyro-Chaldaeans.[20] We cannot avoid stressing that the genocide of the Jews and Gypsies during the Second World War was a genocide of minorities – and non-territorial ones at that. In the Middle East, to take but one example (and there are many), the Bahais are oppressed and repressed as a religious group in the Ayatollah Khomeini's Iran. In Europe itself, the situation of the Hungarian minority in Transylvania (Romania), is one of discrimination and oppression.[21] In Bulgaria the authorities have been engaged in a brutal Bulgarization (forced changing of names, etc.) of the Turkish-speaking minority (about 10 per cent of the population). Outside a handful of democracies,[22] there are few countries where the problems of minorities do not take a discriminatory or oppressive form.

Human rights have found their expression in the Universal Declaration of Human Rights and the 1966 international covenants adopted by the United Nations Organization. The rights of peoples[23] have been interpreted as meaning the right of peoples to enjoy decolonization[24] and the struggle for development. Minority groups (or peoples) have hitherto been excluded from this overall process of formulating rights. Oppression, as we have said already, manifests itself in various forms and in varying degrees. The appropriate solutions are also varied and can only be specific. However, it is essential that rights be granted by the United Nations Organization to ethnic, religious or linguistic minorities. This demand is based on the right to existence and development – that is, on the right to identity and on the religious and/or cultural rights enabling that identity to be perpetuated and developed. The right of minorities to be recognized, not discriminated against *de jure* and *de facto* and protected cannot be separated from human rights. Ultimately, it cannot be dissociated from democracy.*[25]

Notes

1. See in particular the contribution by François Thierry on China and minorities.
2. The right of peoples to revolt is recognized by the Philadelphia Declaration (1776) as well as by the French constitution of 1793 which sees it as 'the most sacred of rights and the most essential of duties'.
3. In sub-Saharan Africa, ethnic cleavages seem to be more important than

---

*It cannot be too deeply regretted that the present situation in Lebanon and particularly the situation of the Christians shows the urgency of the need for thinking about action on the rights and protection of minorities. We hope that we have contributed to that effort and we hope to contribute more in future.

religious cleavages. Theoretically, the federal solution would be best suited there. The effectiveness of the federation would depend on its degree of democracy.

4. The Sudeten Germans in Czechoslovakia; the Hungarian minorities on the one hand, and the Jews, Gypsies and Volga Germans on the other.

5. Jean-François Guilhaudis, *Le droit des peuples à disposer d'eux-mêmes,* (Grenoble, Presses Universitaires de Grenoble, 1976).

6. The Secretary-General of the United Nations stated in Dakar on 4 January 1970: 'As an international organization, the United Nations has never accepted and does not accept and I do not believe it will ever accept the principle of secession of a part of its member states.' The only example of an attempted secession that has succeeded in recent decades is that of Bangladesh — and that was strictly because of Indian military intervention. The only struggles supported by the United Nations Organization are those of 'peoples subject to colonial and foreign domination and to racist regimes for the achievement of their right to self-determination and independence' (resolution of 1 December 1973).

7. Colonial conquests, both British and French, manipulated ethnic differences throughout the imperial period.

8. Article 27 of the 1966 UN Covenant on Civil and Political Rights is concerned with ethnic, religious or linguistic minorities. We feel this definition is less ambiguous and controversial than the expression used in the late nineteenth and early twentieth century, 'national minority'.

9. Assimilation, though no longer fashionable, is also a right.

10. Almost always in a neighbouring country where the ethnic group often has members. Similarly, a very large proportion of the Afghan refugees in Pakistan are Pashtuns who are in a majority in the Pushtu area of Pakistan.

11. There is much talk of the problems of the 'second generation'. What will remain of them in the next one?

12. The collective will to survive may lead to different solutions depending on both the local political context and the spirit of the age. It may lead the group to seek a federal or confederal association, or to autonomy. Secession however cannot be excluded but would certainly be expressed in terms of relationships of force and tests of will. Minorities may also, while retaining their solidarity and collective will to survive, not question their integration in the overall political system.

13. See the Minority Rights Group pamphlet *Selective Genocide in Burundi,* London, MRG.

14. Pierre George, *Géopolitique des minorités,* Paris, PUF, 1984.

15. Jules Deschênes, *Une définition des minorités,* Montreal, 1985.

16. The Kurds in Turkey only have the right to assimilation. They have no official existence as a distinct ethnic and religious group. They are called, euphemistically, 'Mountain Turks'.

17. The Chinese diaspora in Indonesia is generally prosperous and, like the Tamils in Sri Lanka, has in recent decades been the victim of pogroms.

18. The situation in Morocco is similar.

19. Some of them are in fact the majority (Guatemala, etc.).

20. Assyro-Chaldaeans were massacred for being Christians by the Young Turks in 1915, and were the victims of massacres in Iraq in 1933.

21. Minority Rights Group, *The Hungarians in Romania,* London.

22. Japan, whose society is endogenous apart from the Burakumin, discriminates

strictly against it Korean minority. Overall the United States, the product of the largest international migrations in history, is a remarkable success. Given the proportion of foreigners assimilated or integrated in the past century, France, despite a Jacobinism that has little sympathy for regional cultures, is also on the whole a highly integrative society.

23. In this respect, we are a long way from a satisfactory jurisdiction. See particularly the Universal Declaration of the Rights of Peoples, Algiers, 1976.

24. Except for Eritrea and the Western Sahara, all the former European colonies secured independence as states.

25. Bibliographical guide: P. de Azcarate, *League of Nations and National Minorities: An Experiment*, Washington, Carnegie Endowment for International Peace, 1945; Tore Modeen, *The International Protection of National Minorities in Europe*, Abo, Finland, Abo akademi, 1959; Sampat-Mehta, *Minority Rights and Obligations*, Ottawa, Harpell's Press, 1973; Francesco Capotorti, 'Study on the Rights of Persons Belonging to Ethnic, Religious and Linguistic Minorities', in *Report to the United Nations* E/CN.4/sub. 2/384/Rev. 1, June 1977, published in 1979; Benjamin Whitaker (ed.), *Minorities. A Question of Human Rights?*, Oxford, Pergamon Press, 1984; Jules Deschenês, 'A definition of minorities', a study commissioned by the Sub-Commission on Prevention of Discrimination and Protection of Minorities (August 1985 session), Montreal, February 1985; Ali A. Mazrui, *The African Condition*, New York, Cambridge University Press, 1960; Jean-François Guilhaudis, *Le droit des peuples à disposer d'eux-mêmes*, Grenoble, Presses Universitaires de Grenoble, 1976; Pierre George, *Gépolitique des minorités*, Paris, PUF, 1984.

2

The Question of Minorities
in the Order of Law

ALAIN FENET

The law as it pertains to minorities is traditionally regarded in terms of the
protection it might be able to provide for oppressed groups. Certainly this
view is not false: law may indeed provide precious guarantees of form and
substance in the struggle against injustice. But that is only a partial view
and it in fact covers two very different main discourses.

The first of these discourses is humanitarian and liberal: it wants to
bring the benefit of something called law, a neutral aspect of a developed
system, to populations that are maltreated and defenceless. This position
puts much hope in the law while overlooking the relationships of force
that underpin it, and invariably courts disappointment. Often it conceals a
calmly assumed civilizing paternalism. One may wonder, in these cases,
whether for some people, and not only Westerners, the legal argument is
not an avatar of the old discourse of cultural domination: law is being
brought to peoples as culture used to be!

The second discourse is that of the activists. They give a name to a
collectivity, thereby postulating its existence, and then invoke its rights.
Thus inherently held rights are proclaimed of the Breton people, Occitania,
the Jewish community, etc., to mention only cases in France. This stress
on natural law paradoxically results in a statist conception of law; these
rights already held are only advanced to make them into law, that is state
law. Minority groups are said to possess rights but not law, since only the
state can produce law; the group thus only accedes to law through the will
of the state. With this conclusion the discourse of the activists ultimately
links up with the liberal official discourse.

If it is based wholly on the law, the protection of minorities can only
lead to disappointment, confusion and misunderstanding. It seems to me
more fruitful to reverse the postulate and to consider that minorities
possess law and consequently demand rights. In other words, because the
minority is a group, it has a form of jural existence and jural production. I
therefore propose to use law to describe a minority situation, analyse the

minority demand addressed to the state to see whether it has the consistency of law and finally confront this demand with the constraints of the international order. In order to do this successfully, we must first set out the theoretical framework that gives it meaning, based on reference to the jural order.

The Jural Order as a Conceptual Frame of Reference

The question of definitions lies at the heart of scientific analyses and political discussions of the minority question. These include the definition of 'minority' first of all, but also of the concepts of nation, state, homeland, nationality, people, ethnic group, even community and race — concepts that in part overlap and are interwoven.[1] 'Minority' can thus not be defined on its own, but only in relation to other concepts. The difficulty is a real one and partly explains the length and failure of the UN discussions on the subject; but there the difficulty of thinking hides a refusal to act. Of course it is necessary to know what one is talking about, but in these areas the content of a concept results less from a scholarly definition than from the way it is used. The basic concepts that we need to analyse the minority question successfully, concepts of state, minority, nation, can be used operationally, as true analytical tools, if the content given them takes actual practice into account and is hence the object of a broad scientific consensus, and also if they are systematically linked and articulated in a single framework.

Law provides the frame of reference for these concepts but only on the condition that a narrow conception is abandoned and that it is tackled from the notion of jural order.

The Notion of Jural Order

According to a traditional view, law is a body of rules that governs peoples' relations in a given society. This definition clearly shows that in 'the Western view of law, law cannot be separated from the idea of rule.'[2] This emphasis on the normative function overshadows other aspects of the jural, indeed even denies them. In fact, through a logical progression supported by a powerful ideology, law comes to be associated with state coercion. But while the idea of law is of course typically realized in the state, it does not exist only in the state. The notion of jural order makes it possible to clarify this and at the same time stress the basic characteristics of law.

The notion of jural order suggests that law is command, but also that it is organization. As organization, it is something other than a collection of rules. It is a coherent whole, articulated in all its elements, reductive of its own contradictions. It is a formal system structured by a logic and dynamized by a rationality, a single rationality preserving social relations from incoherence. It cannot be dissociated from all the integrative processes by which a society maintains its unity, perpetuates its own order and ensures its survival.[3] Law is thus necessarily conservative: with its own qualifications, linked more or less elaborately, it formulates an established social order that it seeks to defend.[4]

Obviously laws can be changed, but when that happens it means more than simply altering the rules of the system. It is the balance of a whole sub-system, even of the system as a whole, that is more or less upset depending on the extensiveness of the change. Even then this alteration must conform to the central logic of law, 'that logic that constitutes the underlying structure of every jural order'.[5] Otherwise it involves an upheaval implying a restructuring of the whole and a new coherence. This is only attained at the price of a new logic integrating the old and new elements (unless the old law is declared null and void in which case we call this a revolution).[6]

Legal sociologists have established how far the organizational aspect of the law is inseparable from the overall social structure. Law is a product of social relations and finds its profound meaning in those 'fields of intelligibility' constituted by the cultural-economic underpinnings of a given social entity.[7] Law, inseparably linked to the organization of society, does not necessarily depend on the state. The existence of a law of the Eskimo peoples, the Bedouin, the Kanaka, the Gypsies, etc. is no longer denied.[8]

But the notion of jural order also makes it possible to note that law is not necessarily linked to rules either. A society does not merely engender law, it *is* law, because it is an institutionalized relationship. Every social entity is in itself a legal entity. If we consider that a society exists wherever there is interaction of individuals and groups, it is not possible to see society as an envelope within which the jural must be sought.[9] The search for priority here is pointless: 'Law institutes society as much as it is instituted by it.'[10] But this does not mean that there is equivalence between the jural and the social. Not every social interaction is necessarily jural. The jural order imposes a principle of cohesion in order to ensure the survival of the group and the continuance of meanings;[11] the jural consequently signifies stability and constraint.

The gap that exists between the social and the jural is the site of the phenomena of power from which choices and normativeness derive. The fact that this normativeness usually acts diffusely in society, defining the normal and the abnormal, shows that power cannot be perceived as external to society.[12] It constitutes it as much as it is the product of it. Its existence is not arbitrary and its will is in principle intelligible. There is no jural order without an organizing principle and force to keep it operational. A social entity is a complex system of interactions determined by an interplay of forces that dominates and regulates the elements of it. The jural belongs to the order of the instituted and through that of the licit and the obligatory, because it proceeds from an institutor. The relationship of domination, manifested in highly varied forms, is inherent in law. The authority that demands submission may be locatable and named, or invisible, diffuse and implicit; it is always there.

These remarks are valid for any social group, whatever it is and whether or not it is integrated into a larger society. To locate the existence of law is to observe a social entity with an objective and concrete existence, functioning as an organic entity and ensuring its maintenance and development, because it is structured by an effective or symbolic system of power which implies unity.

The notion of jural order so conceived has been elaborated in detail by Santi Romano.[13] According to this author, every social unit is a jural order or, to use his terminology, an institution. Thus understood, an institution is 'a manifestation of the social and not purely individual nature of man' (1975: p. 26). It includes, among other elements, 'several individuals who coexist or follow one another, united by a common or constant interest or by the object, the mission that they are pursuing' (p. 27). In this relative sense, it is 'a closed entity that can be considered in and for itself in that it has an individuality of its own' (p. 27). For Santi Romano, an institution understood as a social unit 'is the primary, original and essential manifestation of law' since 'law consists above all in the establishment and organization of a social entity' (p. 31). 'All force, when it is effectively social and hence organized, is by that very fact transmuted into law' (p. 32). Behind the statement of law, there is first and foremost the authority that states it, which for Santi Romano means that 'law is not, or at least not only, the norm laid down, but the entity that lays it down' (p. 13).

It follows from this analysis that any social unit endowed empirically with a degree of cohesion, whatever the basis on which this cohesion rests, is a jural order. The state order is not the only jural one: any socially organized, coherent and structured unit, whether or not it is recognized by the state, possesses jural character. 'In other words, there are entities which for state law are in part de facto entities whereas considered in themselves, they manifest that institutional character that makes them jural organisms following the conceptions [that we have] developed' (p. 94).

A virtually infinite plurality of jural orders coexist then in a single society, and are related to one another in a variety of ways. A major distinction can be made among them, contrasting those with particular, and hence limited ends, and those with general, potentially unlimited ends. The specificity of the state is not denied compared to the other jural orders which for Santi Romano are constituted by such entities as families, factories, enterprises, churches, sects, boarding schools, sports clubs, criminal associations, etc. On the contrary, variable and complex relationships exist between the state and the other social entities, relationships that Santi Romano surveys using the concept of relevance, which we shall adopt later.

In applying these ideas here, minority groups are envisaged as jural orders. But that is only possible if first the specificity of the state is established, and the concepts of nation and minority are situated in relations to the concept of state.

The State Jural Order: Sovereignty and Legitimacy

The ideas spelled out above are obviously far removed from Kelsen's pure theory of law which asserts that law is a system of norms, as well as from the classical French theory of public law, a particularly developed version of which is to be found in Carré de Malberg. The latter considers that rule of law and state power go hand in hand, so that there is only law through the state. To this he adds that domination, an essential property, is the distinctive feature of the state.[14] For Carré de Malberg, 'in the matter of power, the state is the only power.'[15]

These theories, however, stress that sovereignty is not a particular power, but 'a quality of state power, a quality thanks to which the exercise of this power by the sovereign state depends only on its own will.'[16] The principle of sovereignty is the proclamation by the state of the virtually infinite field of its domination, as well as the exclusion of any other power, either internal or external. By that, the state appropriates to itself the exclusiveness of law.

The internal and external implications of the principle of sovereignty are strongly and effectively linked. Developed in the West essentially in order to ensure the construction of the state, it is the basis of the obligations assumed by the state and thereby of the whole of international law. This operation, clearly conducted from the sixteenth century onwards, borrowed its main features from the old order, in particular from the religious ideology of submission. As Pierre Legendre shows, it established 'the centralizing state as a monotheistic substitute'.[17] All the other social orders gradually lost their jural relevance unless, of course, they were endorsed or taken over by the state, or saw their existence challenged or even denied outright. We know perfectly well that in reality the state is not alone in establishing effective relations of domination. But the nineteenth and twentieth centuries have given the state formidable means of social control which have enabled it to back up its sovereign claims with growing effectiveness. Henceforward, no group, however coherent it may be, is assured of its existence; no interest, however great, is guaranteed if the state has not recognized it in some way — that is, if the state has not integrated it into its jural order.

This presentation of the state calls for three comments.

First, the claim to sovereignty does not arise from nowhere. The creation of the state is an act, real or mythical, by which an authority is instituted, a social unit constituted. In this sense the state is not different from any other jural order. It is no more external to its law than it is external to society.[18]

Second, the claim to sovereignty is not normally deployed arbitrarily. It is limited by the order that enables it to declare itself, before being bound by its own regulations. The state is circumscribed by its own rationality.[19]

Third, the claim to sovereignty secures the consent of men because it is legitimate. It relies on an absolute referent, originally divine and then secularized, which is the basis of supreme power because it puts it beyond attack, beyond debate. It thus brings in what Pierre Legendre calls 'the enigma of an ultimate guarantor to lock up the institution'.[20] But by the same token, sovereignty proceeds from legitimacy, which it cannot escape except by destroying itself. Legitimacy thus derives fundamentally from the jural. It is even the essence of the jural since in the final analysis it is through it that submission is obtained much more than through coercion. 'The ideal state is indeed the one that has the least need to use power to obtain the adhesion of all its people.'[21] Participation in the idea of legitimacy and its concrete representations thus appears as an essential jural act. Participation ensures the cohesion of the group around its basic values, inserts the individual in the state order and strengthens authority. The corollary of this principle is that non-participation, willed or coerced, indicates a marginalization which might possibly express an individual position, but which, when a group is involved, must be analysed as a conflict. That is the situation of a minority.

The Minority Situation: Domination and Legitimacy in the Jural Order

There is no more a minority in itself in socio-political reality than there is in civil or parliamentary law. There is only a minority because there is a majority, in a relationship which can vary. This relationship, so structuring a given social reality, is part of a larger organization from which it cannot be separated. The minorities traditionally considered, ethnic, religious and linguistic, are groups placed in a minority situation by the relationship of force that underlies the global society. It is this relationship that defines them as a minority. The notion of minority is thus not ethnological; it belongs to the politico-legal vocabulary.

In the same way, the minority situation is not fundamentally a matter of numbers. The relationship of domination is not necessarily established on a numerical basis.[22] The example of South Africa (an extreme case, but not the only one) shows that populations can be in the numerical majority and yet placed in a politico-legal relationship of being a minority. Moreover, a minority group in a given whole, like the Kurdish people, may be an overwhelming majority in its own territory. The numbers factor may, of course, have considerable practical implications but these do not reveal the profound reality of the minority situation. It is always 'the objective relationship to power that makes the minority'.[23] A minority is a group specifically dominated, established in a situation of dependence or inferiority by an act of power that designates, categorizes and removes. Any group can thus be placed in a minority situation.

It thus appears essential to see that the category 'minority' is created by a determinate social structuration and not by more or less 'natural' signs characterizing the group in some distinctive manner. These signs are erected into criteria in order to name and classify. Certainly, this or that sign may be a real factor of identity, 'but the concept of minority is, in itself, independent of this factor'.[24] A very real difference only takes on meaning in the political arena that designates it for this purpose. That difference, therefore, may fade away, even disappear, and yet the minority can continue to exist if the act that designated it is endlessly repeated.

We thus arrive at those extreme limiting cases in which racism 'constitutes even artificially a non-existing ethnic group ... with very assorted individuals that did not constitute one',[25] in which apartheid *designates* a Black man under a white skin, and an ancient discrimination makes a Japanese into a Burakumin.[26]

These analyses do not seek to deny the existence of peculiar characteristics and specific identities. Factors of differentiation work on humanity in complex ways in both time and space. Delicately shaded identities result from the interaction of the diversities of language, religion, culture and genetic inheritance within the framework of determinate social organizations. The point here is that the act of power that makes diversity into an inferiority transforms a group into a minority.

It is not therefore difficult to understand that the question of minorities may appear to be of 'frightening complexity' and that there is no universally accepted definition.[27] Each minority is indeed a specific case since it is the result of an act of power designed to secure the exercise of domination in a given society. But by the same token, this approach to the problem does not mean that analysis must get lost in the many specific cases of minority populations; the analysis must concentrate on the process of making a minority, the logic of which lies in the foundations of political organization. These are expressed in the statements of legitimacy that assert in the name of what, how and for what ends people are to be commanded. The content of the legitimizing principle in a given society reveals a minority in the negative. A group is in a minority situation when its existence is not covered by the statements of legitimacy. It is outside the justifications and ends of power. Unamenable to the argument of legitimacy, it is by its very existence a challenge for authority. The response of power-holders to this social reality that they are unable to control depends both on how far they perceive it as a threat and what use they can make of it. The history of the principle of traditional Western legitimacy that we shall briefly outline shows how each type of political organization creates its minorities.

In the ancient city-state there was no minority. Based on participation in a common religious origin, the group had total cohesion. Breach of the social bond was a sacrilege, sanctioned by elimination or its equivalent, ostracism. Rome reconciled this requirement with its imperial expansion through a polytheism hospitable to the deities of subjugated peoples. This solution ran up against the obstinate monotheism of the Jewish people. As the first minority in the Western political tradition, the Jew has remained down to our own days, actually or potentially a 'counter-type frightening by his very existence, since he typifies, in any exclusive system, the other that one tries to exclude or absorb'.[28]

The Jew was joined by the Christian until the Christianization of the empire transformed the parameters of the problem. From then on, legitimacy proceeded from the Christian religion and the church claimed to grant it or at least to authenticate it. Power was held by the emperor or a monarch who proclaimed himself emperor in his kingdom, and was held by Christian divine right. Religious discipline ensured social cohesion and political submission. Europe began to develop linguistic and cultural traits that were more and more diversified, but Christian unity knew only one minority, the Jew, who was not to be massacred ('a monstrous idea', according to St Bernard) but who had to be subjugated (and was thus luckier than the Muslim).[29]

The division of Christianity and the political break-up of Europe increased the number of religious minorities as the principle of '*cuius regio, eius religio*' enshrined by the Treaty of Westphalia was put into effect.

Finally, the slow rise of the bourgeoisie and its coming to power involved a restructuring of political and administrative institutions, and above all a new base of legitimacy. God was replaced by the nation, divine right by national sovereignty, and subjects by citizens. This new basis of power appeared liberatory since it proclaimed the rights of man along with the rights of the nation. Yet it inaugurated an era of increased violence in inter-state relations and led to the appearance of countless minorities. The worldwide diffusion of the nation-state model through the continuous effect of colonization and decolonization, and its endorsement at the United Nations as the sole legitimate mode of governing men, constitute the ultimate stage of Western political hegemony. The result has been a globalization of the problem of minorities; its relevance in the Third World is the reflection of the actual results secured by the nation-building enterprises embarked on there.

National Unity: Legitimacy and Exclusion

The concept of nation is the subject of various interpretations that are forever dragging it into the field of ethnology. This deviation is the source of profound and sometimes deliberate conceptual and political misunderstandings. Yet the worldwide diffusion of the national ideology and the model of the nation-state ought to constitute a powerful conceptual constraint. Placed in a historical perspective, the word nation has nothing to do with ethnology, but belongs to the language of law and politics. In this vocabulary, the nation is a signifier. It expresses the new idea of legitimacy elaborated by the bourgeoisie in its rise to power in order to subvert ideologically and soon replace the feudal-monarchical order. For that it subjected the concept of nation to a reworking that found its most complete formulation in the French Revolution.[30] The nation is thus an idea expressing a particular political relationship, a way of linking people to power without reference to the divine. It lays down an *a priori* principle of political unity among people who are distinguished from, even opposed to, one another otherwise. As a representation of unity, it is a value in itself producing a higher degree of acceptance of power. But it is also charged with the basic values of society, which power thus seizes to its own advantage. It is then an idea, but an active idea: the nation points to a future, a project of building, which becomes reality through the action of political forces and the work of time.[31]

Since the eighteenth century, then, the nation has ceased to be seen as the place where one is born, or a province as under the *ancien régime*, or an ethnic group or tribe or so-called 'natural' community differentiated by language, religion, genetic inheritance or any other factor.[32] It may indeed be nourished by these agents of solidarity and rest on marks of identity or networks of social relationships. But it always differentiates itself from them because it expresses the modern idea of political unity. National feeling is the feeling of political unity, an intimate allegiance to the community and the authority that organizes it into a nation.

This amounts to saying that the nation calls forth the state in the same way that the state invokes the nation. 'In this jural sense, the nation is no longer only one of the constituent elements of the state, but it is supremely *the* constituent element of the state, in so far as it identifies itself with it.'[33] The unity of the community demands the unity of the government; it refers to a centre from which power emanates. Power has the task of maintaining unity, of continuously ensuring the cohesion of all the elements of the social order. Nationalism describes a never assuaged desire for an ever closer unity at the same time as the exaltation of national separateness. In the nationalist universe, the uniformity of individuals and the veneration they have for power condition the happiness of the population.

What therefore is decisive is the way this unity is conceived, organized and maintained. The concrete content of the national idea, in which language often occupies a privileged position, constitutes in each particular case the principle of unity.[34] At the same time it is in this principle that the factor of exclusion lies, the factor that places people in a minority situation. It is thus fundamentally on this principle that the effort must be directed in order to work lastingly in favour of minorities.

The Minority as a Jural Order

Relating the minority situation to the conceptual framework outlined above implies first of all that the minority constitutes a social entity, next that as such it forms a jural order, and finally that this order is in a particular relationship to that of the state.

A Minority is a Social Entity

A minority is a social entity because it is a collective being, a group, which manifests itself in a collective subjectivity.

The jural approach to the minority question stresses that a minority is a dominated group. Before being a minority this group existed as a social entity. This does not mean to imply that it was a closed unit, with sharp boundaries and closed to the world outside. The social groups that make up a society are composed in various ways, more or less loosely, on varying bases and for various purposes. They are articulated on one another, overlap one another, even are tangled up in one another. A minority is one of these groups, part of a global society. It is not an undifferentiated and transitory relationship among individuals, but a specifically constituted group. There is only a minority because there is a group, and thus only when there is a group. This point is fundamental: the social unit constituted by a group may be sectional, partial or all-embracing, established on one or several particular factors, but it is always the product of a solidarity among the members. On this basis, the group is a relatively autonomous social reality, endowed with a life of its own, distinct from that of the individuals composing it.

As a group, a minority considered for itself thus exists less by virtue of its specific characteristics than through the unity that results from it. Any social fact can be a factor of unity. In this area, nothing is natural or necessary; the raw datum is less important than the instituting function that it may eventually perform. Some characteristics are of course in this respect more effective than others because they involve intense relationships among individuals and above all because they are easily charged with multiple and complex meanings, induce particular social practices, designate others and other places. But therein lies the essential point: this happens in the institutive operation or practice to the extent that the particular characteristic is made a signifier, charged with social and political implications that go beyond it. A social group is first and foremost a preferential system of communication.

These comments are as valid for language or religion as they are for any factor of solidarity. They do not involve any devaluation of those groups that concern us particularly, the minorities traditionally labelled 'ethnic, religious and linguistic'. At most they indicate the danger of deeming them to possess a particular essence because, for example, they are claimed to be 'natural' communities and so escape the conditions in which any social group exists. We all know that a language, a notorious factor of close, regular and complex relations, can be dropped by its speakers for all sorts of reasons and lose its function as a social bond. Conversely, a specific feature that is apparently of no great importance can become an effective factor of cohesion and engender a social entity; later it may be the object of a reverse process of banalization sending the members of the group back to their individuality.[35]

In this constant interplay, the relationship with the outside world is always an important feature; it is a component of the production of identity. This component is essential, if not primary, when we are dealing with a minority, that is a group subjected to a relationship of domination. It is very often this relationship that pushes the members of a minority to unity. As we have already pointed out, the dominant group is sometimes even strong enough to create out of nothing a group to satisfy its need for domination.[36]

If the factors of solidarity have a relative value, there is nevertheless a distinction among the groups that they produce, between on the one hand functional groups, and on the other, suprafunctional groups or global communities. In order to describe the latter the notion of *ethnos* has come to be accepted, including in Europe, but at the cost of a diversification of its content. In France particularly one school of thought which has done much work for the defence of minorities sees in the *ethnos* the true nation, defined principally in terms of language. 'Here, the *ethnos* describes the body of people speaking the same language and more precisely the same mother tongue.'[37] There are too many objections to this use of the concept of *ethnos* for it to be accepted.[38] Sociologists prefer the expression ethnic group or community. By that they mean a relatively stable socio-cultural unit performing an unspecified number of functions, bound together by a language, often linked to a territory, and derived actually or allegedly from a system of kinship. In this sense, 'the ethnic community is an extremely old collective reality, naturally much earlier than the appearance of a political formation like the nation, earlier too than the appearance of social classes.'[39] From the ethnic community to the nation there is then not necessarily a change of community, but there is a change of project. There is a movement from the order of tradition to a future-oriented modern political enterprise. The collective consciousness changes nature, and it is that that gives its true identity to the group.

We are thus not devaluing the ethnic minority by emphasizing that like any community it only exists in so far as it constitutes a collective subjectivity.[40] The particular traits function as 'atoms of information', in Jacques Berque's expression.[41] To this extent, they engender a feeling of belongingness and play an effectively instituting role. The feeling of a specific identity thus involves the feeling of belonging to the group. Conversely, the abandonment or devaluation of particular signs indicate the decline of the feeling of belongingness. Without this element of collective consciousness, a group does not exist. In the case of a minority, 'it is at best a matter of a group in the process of being assimilated or of a potential minority'.[42] On the basis of this consciousness that values the group and its distinctive signs, an action of defence and survival can be embarked upon. A group only maintains itself over time, especially if it is in a minority situation, through the attachment of individuals to the group.[43] This is shown in an enormous amount of everyday behaviour. It can then be accepted that 'it is logical to conclude that their general attitude should be viewed as a clear affirmation of their will to preserve and develop their own characteristics.'[44]

This self-affirmation is particularly necessary to resist the brutal processes of assimilation; its absence always endangers the group. The group may, for example, fall apart if the pressures that have strongly contributed to its creation cease. The identity factor was then too external to the actual situation of individuals to maintain in any lasting way a sense of belongingness. In the same way, the existence of a minority is threatened if leaving the group appears to major social segments within it or to a growing number of individuals as the condition of a better life. 'The paradox of any cultural minority ... is that the reasons for dissolving itself may appear more convincing than the reasons for maintaining itself.'[45]

We then reach what J.-P. Chrétien says about Africa, but also what others say about France: that ethnic identity is posed in terms of a value of commitment. Being Breton, Jewish or Basque in modern-day France means *wanting to be* Breton, Jewish or Basque.[46] Identity is not a sign but a practice. If it is not, the signs merely testify to a past and degenerate into nostalgic folklore, an object of voyeurism for tourists; in reality, the individuals have then ceased to make it the site of their identity. But they may decide to return to it. Some members or classes of the minority may throw themselves into a movement to reappropriate the signs and then invest them with new meanings. This is an indication of a change of strategy on their part in an attempt to preserve a threatened social position. The new commitment to the original group reveals a crisis and the means through which a solution is sought.[47]

It is thus not possible to ignore the economic, social and political aspects, whether internal or external to the group, which catch individuals in a complex network of relations and determine which identity they assert. In the defence of a language or a culture, there are many other things than the conquest or the preservation of a legal status. There is the overall existential situation of individuals. If we fail to acknowledge it, it is not possible to grasp the motivations that drive the members of the group 'to this rather strange, rather mysterious activity that consists in maintaining oneself as an identifiable and distinct group'.[48]

However, from the perspective of minorities as jural orders we have adopted here, the question to be considered is simply whether the group's capacity to react to external influences enables it to maintain its unity and cohesion, to keep up the solidarity among its members. The feeling of belongingness is not enough, it must on occasion be capable of leading to an active commitment.[49] The character of the individual is a factor that might be important. More decisive is the capacity the group has to influence and inspire respect. The capacity for social influence ensures a control over the behaviour of individuals and perhaps even a sanction, even if this latter consists only of disapproval. It secures submission to the group norms and respect for the obligations binding the group. This behaviour must enhance respect in the individual. It must express more than his conformism and constitute a way to social integration. Then the minority constitutes a dynamic social entity which can be analysed as a jural order.

A Minority is a Jural Order

We have seen that there was a close link, but not an equivalence, between the jural order and the social entity, the jural order crystallizing the identity of the group in its vital core, on its essential principles. Having established the minority as a social entity, we must now explain in what way it is a jural order. We shall do this from the two dimensions of the notion of jural order: organization and norm.

The internal organization of the group manifests its jural nature. It makes it organically into an institution.[50] It unites the group by ensuring the maintenance of the social bond. It stresses the signs of belongingness and their carriers. But it may also take on social needs going beyond the strict requirements of group definition: organization enriches the content of unity by adding various extra features to the initial singularity.[51] The group thus only ensures its character as a jural order from the time when an authority has been formed within it that incarnates its unity and pursues its achievement, and which to that end creates institutions and reminds individuals of their obligations. This is true whatever the nature of the group and the basis of its social bond, whether this bond is sectional and narrowly defined or general and indefinite. Authority can thus manifest itself in a great variety of forms, diffuse or clearly identified, institutionalized and recognized, or self-proclaimed and debated, unified or pluralistic. But it is never the outcome of a sort of natural necessity. It is produced by the phenomena of power that is manifested in the group. The group is a site of forces but it is also true that its very identity is decided by power.

All projects aiming to ensure the survival of a minority group and to strengthen its resistance envisage the establishment of a common reference point, enabling the social entity to be organized. We need, says Robert Laffont writing of Occitanism, 'a specific organ for action and reflection'.[52] This capacity for specific organization indicates the internal social dynamism of the group. The strength that is invested in it makes the group a real social space and not a mere illusory, mythical and dangerous point of reference. In a political analysis, it is important to specify what social categories are involved in the group and incarnated in the signs; in a jural analysis, it is enough to take note of the existence of an order. Conversely, the weakening and disappearance of the authority structures indicate the loss of respect for the internal stakes and the dilution of the relationships of force specific to the group.

This observation makes it possible to avoid two pitfalls. First, it preserves minority groups from idealization. The reality of the domination to which they are subjected does not make them into the last refuges of the Good and the Just. Like any instituted social group, a minority is a political space in which a power is exercised, extremely variable in nature and character, but sometimes unjust and even cruel. In some contexts, the reality of that domination is even a decisive factor in eroding the group. When departure from the group is experienced as liberation and progress, then assimilation is not a loss of identity but a positive and exclusive transfer of allegiance. Therein lies one of the essential aspects of the success of French nationalist ideology; of course it calls for assimilation, but it does so into a republic with a civil code and the rights of man.

The second pitfall to avoid is, conversely, devaluing the internal life of the group. It is through its internal vitality, its capacity to regulate conflicts, and through the energy that is invested in it that the group maintains and adapts itself. A group with indefinite functions such as an ethnic group is by its very nature a site of conflicts which are sometimes well concealed by the traditional culture or the mechanisms of external defence. But the external constraint may precisely have the effect of binding the group closer together by compelling it to seek a new equilibrium, a new organization of authority, a new definition of its unity.[53]

In the final analysis, as a group, a minority possesses an internal life structured by its own relationships of force. This practical regulation of social life on the vital bonds of unity makes the minority a jural order. This order may be loose, but it still exists so long as effective representations of the unity in images of authority subsist.[54] The individual faithful to the group bows before an authority, submits himself to a word held to be legitimate, and in so doing makes an act of allegiance to the collectivity as an institution. Jural behaviour is summed up in submission to the community before it is detailed in obedience to norms.

The norms internal to the minority play an essential role in the processes that maintain it as a unit. These norms derive from the social relations instituted in the group; they necessarily express the contradictions underlying the organization of the group. They take many different forms: residual local laws surviving the establishment of the modern state not only in Africa or among the Indians and Eskimos, but also in Europe in particularly close-knit communities;[55] the law of indigenous peoples; the law of nomad peoples, the Gypsies in Europe, essentially customary in character; the law linked to a code of honour and modes of social organization, whose formulation is hardly explicit and whose visibility is low.

These norms are areas and functions limited according to the nature of the social bond. They may sometimes appear very rough, not very jural, particularly in groups that are not ethnic ones. There is thus a temptation to refuse to see them as law or at most to see only the rules governing ethnic groups as law. These two viewpoints can be dismissed.

It is not necessary to deal here with the jural nature of relationships other than those ordained by the state.[56] It is more important to mention the distinction often made between what is seen as true law, or law imposed by the state, and what is seen as a mere jural system, or sub-law or popular law.[57] We shall not use this distinction. It runs the risk of being understood pejoratively, and above all it is not necessary in terms of the notion of jural order we have used. A jural order in fact is only partial in relation to what it is not. It is complete for the needs of the social group from which it derives. It is consistent with the partial ends of the group, logically linked to the basic bond uniting the group. In terms of what concerns us here, it is law.

The viewpoint that grants a jural character only to ethnic communities must also be rejected. It rests on the thesis that only natural communities with indefinite functions can produce law by reason of their capacity for forming a complete jural order. The jural character is said to belong to necessary communities and not to sectional or voluntary groupings. This way of seeing things is generally inspired by conceptions of natural law aiming at singling out ethnic groups among the set of minorities and according a particular legitimacy to actions carried out in their favour. This is a respectable concern which does not, however, take reality into account. The jural character of voluntary associations cannot reasonably be denied.[58] In addition the distinction between voluntary associations and necessary associations seems to be altogether relative. What is to be made of the gangs of 'Bogota kids' outside which survival is far from certain? What of the ban on apostasy imposed by Islam and the indelible character of baptism in canon law? Here we must follow the method given by Santi Romano, according to which it is the objective law of the social entity that determines its necessary or voluntary character and not the other way round. 'Any qualification given it from another viewpoint is jurally meaningless.'[59] Consequently ethnic groups are not the only ones to be amenable to jural analysis.

Yet the argument has its *raison d'être*. It aims at preventing an extension of the notion of minority beyond its traditionally accepted limits (so-called ethnic, religious and linguistic minorities). In order to take advantage of the kudos accruing to identification as a minority, activists have proclaimed women, the young, the old, and homosexuals as minorities. We must of course fight against any unthinking use of the notion of minority which would empty it of its content, that is, ignore its key characteristic of domination specifically exercised over an established social entity. Ethnic groups certainly have the advantage of easily demonstrating and maintaining the character of a social entity. But knowing whether any particular social category constitutes a minority calls for a shaded response, following the approach suggested by Santi Romano. Once it is established that a particular social category is in a situation of specific domination, it is still necessary that it be capable of a movement of institutionalization, or even that it wants it. The response is given by the practice of those concerned who may or may not give themselves a unitary reference, organizations, a list of demands, a draft statute. A group of children, an old people's home, a women's circle may constitute an institution, a limited jural order, but neither children, pensioners nor women form social entities and thus are not minorities. They would be considered minorities according to the criteria outlined above if their demands were formalized and entered into institutions of reference shared by the whole of the category. The French feminist movements have perhaps gone as far as possible in this direction, but they have failed to reach it.[60] Their demands aim to obtain individual rights, not collective ones. What is at issue is the fate of individuals, not the fate of a social entity.

From these remarks, a double series of practical proposals can be extracted. First, demanding rights for a group amounts to asserting the existence of this group as a jural order, that is as a social reality. That requires spelling out the effective bonds and consequent group unity and locating the phenomena of power which are exercised in the group in precise or diffuse manifestations of authority over individuals. Second, when a historically locatable group no longer has the articulations and wellsprings necessary to constitute a social order, it is no longer *ipso facto* a jural order. The problems are then no longer those of the relationships between two jural orders but between an imposed jural order and individuals. The problematic to be adopted is no longer that of the rights of the group since there is no longer any law of the group: it is the problematic of human rights.

The Minority Situation is a Particular Relationship Between the State Order and the Order of a Group

As a social entity within an overarching whole, a minority is a jural order specifically dominated by the order of the state as a result of the non-inclusion of the group's values in the idea of legitimacy. Each jural order is inspired by a rationality which is itself underpinned by values. The gap between the jural rationality and the values of each order determines how far they are compatible. There cannot be conflict within a jural order, duality of rationality, or contradictions between established values.

The minority situation translates concretely this creation of a gap between one order and another. It can be manifested by a whole variety of practices on the part of the state — from mere indifference to the most savage repression — that depends on the compatibility of the two jural orders as assessed by the rulers and on those rulers' strictly political goals.

Indifference may correspond to a small gap in jural rationality. It may also reflect the lack of concern on the part of the government *vis-à-vis* the main features of the minority order that seem irrelevant to the needs of domination; it ignores them or tolerates them as simple facts. It may also mask the confidence that the government has in the integrative virtues of its own jural order.[61] Indifference may thus equally be analysed as tolerance or as a soft policy of assimilation. The various techniques of repression, on the other hand, rest on a declaration that all or part of the social bond uniting the dominated group is illegitimate. But their function is equally ambivalent. They can as well aim at making the group disappear as a constituted social entity — either by eliminating its members or by destroying the social bond — as at creating or keeping it in a minority situation of open oppression for the benefit of the dominant order. In this case, the difference is maintained as a stain and to function as a sign; it could not be tolerated as a source of law. But the illegitimacy decreed by the state is not in itself sufficient to make jural orders disappear; oppressed social entities subsist as jural orders 'so long as they have life, that is so long as they are constituted, have an internal organization and represent an order'.[62]

The members of minority groups thus appear at the intersection of contradictory injunctions emanating on the one hand from the social entity of origin and on the other from the dominant order. This situation is recent in Africa, where the introduction of the nation-state on the Western model has created a situation in which 'the rights of minorities are a burning issue' since 'in most developing countries ... the assimilation of all elements of the population into the mainstream of the nation is a basic objective.'[63] In Europe, the minority situation sometimes appears today in a rather attenuated form. The practice of states, resting on a democratic national ideology and effective mechanisms of integration, gives some credibility to their claim to be the sole jural order. Moreover many European territorial minorities now have the traits of a jural order only in a weakened form. The policy of putting groups into a minority situation has here almost reached its goal of destroying social entities otherwise instituted. But even in a democratic state, so long as a group subsists, there is always constraint in the relationship that the state order maintains with the minority order, in the sense that the existence of the group or its capacities for autonomous development are denied.[64]

This relationship, always involving constraint between the two jural orders, does not necessarily contain only constraint. Various factors may come into play in this respect relating, of course, to the state order and also to the behaviour of the members of the minorities themselves. As a group, the minority is only one locus of identification among others in the overall society. Society is the scene of interactions that are the more numerous and complex the more the group has a reduced sectional function. These interactions are also favoured by the democratic character of the state or by the attractive qualities of the larger society. The member of a minority is in the state order and benefits from it in his status as citizen, producer, consumer, etc. But the group may also eventually benefit from it. It may indeed find in public services and the territorial administration of the state the means to organize and create instruments of development. 'A department for the Basque country!' is a demand by the Basque movement in France. This relative ambivalence of the state structures doubtless only applies in democratic states. In the French case, it has to be admitted that this ambiguity has always been under-exploited — a fact that can be partly explained by the behaviour of agents of the state and partly by the submission of the peoples and their representatives to the national ideology imposed from the centre.[65]

In the final analysis, there are no simple recipes or Manichaean formulas for acting for the benefit of members of minorities. What has to be done is to modify a minority situation, that is, to act on the existing relationship between the state order and the order of the group under consideration. Action may thus be directed to a whole variety of objects situated both in the state order and in the minority order, the objective being always to establish a more favourable relationship for the minority. The establishment of this relationship implies a respect for consistency that we must now explore in discussing the minority demand directed to the state.

The Minority Demand

The minority demand addressed to the state is bound to a consistency that flows from the fact that the group is part of the global order. Whether this is the existing order or an order to be established, what is involved is always the same whole caught in a single logic, because it is structured by a predominant field of forces. Demanding rights means accepting that the demand take its place within a larger order to whose rules it must conform at least in part and whose basic constraints it must accept altogether. This has major implications both for the formulation and the content of the demand.

The Formulation of the Demand

The demand is a moment of truth to the extent that it emanates from the group itself and denounces the reality of the group's domination. It is the word of truth of the group, but it is also a test of truth for the group.

The demand is the word of truth because only the group is competent to state the type of relations that suit it in the state. It cannot do it by proxy. It is even the basic act by which a group begins to emerge from its minority situation. By making the demand, the group is rejecting the definitions and limits that enclose it in its dominated situation. It is at last speaking out. It used not to have the right to, or, if it did, it could only do so in the manner authorized by the majority. By its autonomous demand, the minority reveals its existence and its potential power. The demand shocks since it makes visible and asserts what the official discourse concealed or downplayed. It causes fear since it marks the failure of the illusory attempt to reduce the group to powerlessness pursued by government.[66] It marks the appearance of a 'problem': Blacks in the United States, Jewish communities in the Soviet Union, Kurdish, Kabyle, etc. There is only a minority problem because there is a minority movement; and the problem is in the measure and the image of this movement.

The word externalizes the collective awareness. By making a demand, the group defines itself in its own eyes as much as in the eyes of others. It embarks on a practice of self-affirmation in which it is seeking itself. In societies where the integration of minorities has long since been achieved and the assimilation of some of them is not far from being completed, as in France, the demand becomes a factor determining identity. Having become a choice, the identity is in the movement of individuals and not in the markers, the traces of which disappear and the meaning of which is erased.[67] The demand then appears also as a test of truth for the group.

This test is judged in the representativeness of those who speak on behalf of the group and in their capacity to express the reality of the group's experience.

The question of the representativeness of the spokesmen is at first sight a complicated one. On top of the diversity of minority situations there is that of the identity strategies pursued by the groups. Thus for a religious minority, the ecclesiastical institution can legitimately perform this role, but it can just as well give way to any other community institution of a political or cultural character. Conversely, the role of the clergy in the defence of linguistic minorities to which it ministers is well known, especially in Europe. In any case, it is clear that representativeness is always relative and that it varies over time, sometimes considerably, sometimes very quickly.

But beyond its status, the representativeness of the spokesman is tied up with the content of what he says. This can change so long as it describes faithfully the reality of the social entity. That relates less to an institutional description than to an analysis of the political situation within the group. It is a matter of knowing who wants to assert what and can impose himself in the group.[68] This question is often raised for minorities held closely in the grip of traditional relationships that come into contact with modernity. It is also important for territorial minorities in modern societies, France in particular. The fact is that the 'nationalitarian' movements active among these minorities want to reconstitute living social entities, reclaiming bits of the heritage but above all recreating a new identity. This voluntarism is praiseworthy and has a significant impact.[69] But it does raise questions. Why this desire for affirmation, this quest for identity? Of what is it made? With what goals? The replies vary. For some, it represents the temptation to return to their origins in order to flee the anxiety created by the loss of meaning following major social changes that have not been mastered locally.[70] Others see it as the crisis of the provincial petty bourgeoisie seeking its future outside the integrative mechanisms of the state.[71] Still others see in it concrete manifestations of a distortion between the state and the nation, the state losing its national content to become an imperialist agent.[72]

These lines of analysis are usually rejected by the nationalist movements because they do not like these upsetting questions to be raised. It is simpler to postulate the existence of a people and to attribute to it a national dimension. This ideological approach, which is particularly at work in Corsica, is an evasion which serves to mask the fact that the social entity no longer has its previous alleged coherence and dynamism. The ideology of unity does not serve in this case to legitimize an established practice productive of identity; at best it aims at reconstituting politically new conditions for such a practice.[73] Yet nationalism among members of minorities is easy to understand. It offers a radical solution to the question of liberation through repeating the model of the nation-state. It bases the demand on values proclaimed to be universal, and which can thus be opposed to those of others. Nonetheless in most cases it is anachronistic and politically questionable.

Yet there exist other ways of enabling a minority to escape from its condition and accede to universality in the global society and equality in the law of the state. But it has to show realism. If nationalism is to be rejected then a set of demands must be formulated that accurately describe the reality of the minority order to enable it to be taken into consideration by the state and in order to obtain the means of making that order function better. That presupposes that choices are made within the group on the basis of clear images of its future, but also that these choices are adopted by the real forces guiding the group. If this is done, the formulation of the demand leads to a process of unification in the group which enables it to enter usefully into conflict with the imposed order. This opens up the field of political struggle which supposes allies and a strategy.

This strategy is not directed against society or against the state. But it does take place *in* society and the state to which the members of the minority are attached by a multitude of varied bonds. The strategy is argued out in a shared universe, partly on the basis of shared values and common points of reference. This shared universe, real and imagined, gives a practical meaning to the demand, and makes it into an operational political instrument. It largely determines its success. The demand, a sign of rationality, is thus also a mark of confidence in the majority and of hope in the state. Whether this trust is well-founded is, of course, another matter which requires an analysis of each case. But one paradoxical consequence must be stressed: by affirming its autonomous demands, the group emphasizes and strengthens the bonds linking it to the society as a whole.

On the jural level, this is reflected in a demand for an absolute guarantee of individual equality, a prerequisite to rather than the content of the demand. Equality is the very content of the demand, when discrimination has as its only object the maintenance of the group through preventing its members from dispersing into the global society. But it is a prerequisite if the group wants to maintain its existence. Equality then expresses positively the fact that individuals belong to a plurality of social entities; it enables each individual to enjoy this multiple bonding which is abstracted in the quality of citizen.[74] That is why non-discrimination as an approach to the minority question does not conflict with protection through the granting of special rights. In a national society, equality is the very basis of the integration of one order by another. There is always the risk, of course, that integration in a state order might lead to assimilation through the spontaneous action of the dominant relations and influences. A group that is gradually losing its functions loses its *raison d'être*. Demanding the enjoyment of full rights in a given system implies participation in the totality of social life and consequently the risk of a high frequency of individual assimilation. The first right of a member of a minority is thus paradoxically the right to assimilation, because it is the implicit condition of positive exercise of his differentness. Otherwise, it is back to the logic of enclosure, which is alien to democracy and carried to its absurd and odious logical conclusion in the system of apartheid. This enclosure may be clearly an issue in a power play within the group; it may more simply be a utopian aim of 'returning to the sources', burying oneself in the protective embrace of one's origins. It is difficult to see how it can have a free run outside democratic ideals.[75]

On the basis of non-discrimination can be built a particular demand, the content of which expresses otherness.

The Content of the Demand

The demand aims to secure recognition of the characteristics of the minority jural order by the state order. It asks that the state cease denying or persecuting the minority order, and cease too ignoring it, treating it as a simple fact of life, or giving it a character that it does not give it itself; it calls for a positive relationship between the two orders.

Santi Romano's ideas suggest how this relationship can be established. He argues that a sovereign order does not necessarily have to deny the jural value of another order. 'It is difficult to see why,' he says, 'it could not recognize it as a jural order, even if only up to a certain point, for some purposes and with whatever status it sees fit to grant it.' In order to describe this operation, Santi Romano puts forward the concept of *jural relevance*, defined thus: 'For there to be jural relevance, the existence, content and effectiveness of an order must conform to the conditions laid down by another order: this order is only valid for that other jural order on the basis laid down by this latter.'[76]

Demanding rights for a minority group thus amounts to defining in what ways the minority is relevant for the state order. It is a matter of discovering a new legal relationship by which the dominated or ignored order becomes a recognized and subordinate order. A relationship of exclusion becomes a hierarchical relationship. This integration of the minority order into the state order cannot be done arbitrarily. It implies the acceptance of the fundamental constraints of the state order, which usually evolves slowly, barring major crises or revolutions. Relevance is the organization of a dependence on the demands of a dominant jural rationality and in the formal articulations of coherent legal arrangements. This operation is all the easier where the two orders share a common universe, rest on similar values and have numerous links between them.

Subjected to these conditions, relevance may be only partial. Some traits of the minority order may remain ignored or even combatted by the state. It may also be impossible: in recognizing the minority order, the state cannot undermine the coherence of its own jural order. There cannot be a contradiction institutionalized within a single system of law.[77] But jural orders may turn out to be incompatible, with their rationalities mutually exclusive, because they reflect worldviews that are too far apart or are based on opposing values or even on different rationalities. It is impossible to ignore the fact that 'jural rationality is above all the expression of a frame of reference.'[78] In other words, it goes to the heart of state domination: to the idea of legitimacy. Of course this can become modified as the political and cultural balances within society change, but these modifications are slow and lead to enrichments and shifts of the jural rationality, which in any event always remains unique. Rapid or total upheavals can only result from severe political struggles leading to new principles of legitimacy. Generally,

If those who proclaim the law see their freedom of decision limited, that relates to the necessity of respecting the unity of rationality of the system. Only the creator of a system *ab initio* can impose a new rationality, by virtue of which the old law can be declared null and void. This is what revolutionaries do after the establishment of a new social order.[79]

If the demand of a minority group fits into the adaptations of which the system is capable, the state can satisfy it without too much difficulty. But if we consider that a minority group is an order not covered by legitimacy, we can then see that total acceptance of its demand requires more than the adoption of a few new legal texts. What is at stake in this case is the suppression of the minority situation, which implies a modification of the content of the legitimacy, that is of the national consensus. These new political conditions are reflected in a wholesale rearrangement of the law of the state on the basis of an updated jural rationality. This results from an accommodation of the jural rationalities of the orders involved. In this operation, the established rationality of the state is likely to play the major role.

To take the French case, it will be agreed that the rights of man, the French language and the centrality of the state constitute the core of the national consensus, the fundamental bonds which underpin and govern political unity. Consequently, short of a new definition of itself, the republic cannot accept either private vengeance like the vendetta, or the public punishment in the Gypsy order, or the excision of girls, or Koranic rules relating to the status of women. In the same way, it can only, short of a new national definition, contemplate no more than at most a territorial bilingualism for the linguistic minorities.

Thus in most cases, the minority demand supposes a compromise that partly allows the minority situation to continue to exist. This compromise is both an opportunity and a risk for the minority since it may devitalize it. It eliminates open oppression, but by lowering the group's defences it always borrows more from the dominant rationality than it does from that of the minority order. The minority order may thus gradually lose its unifying frames of reference. If the group does not succeed in adapting itself to this new definition of itself brought about by the compromise, the latter then only opens the way to assimilation by way of organized folklore. The law of the state is necessarily an instrument of the integration of society in conformity with the idea that it has of itself. The complete suppression of the minority situation implies that the society does not think of itself without the group in question, in a new idea of itself. The preservation of the difference then becomes a part of the national consensus and the state is at its service. This undertaking soon runs up against the logic of the unitary state. Here the elements that make up the national bond can be reduced or expanded; they cannot be heterogeneous, inconsistent or without articulations. This requirement, essential to the production of a unifying jural rationality, does not arise, or rather arises in other, less rigorous terms, in the case of systems based on federalism. There is probably something permanent about minority situations because of the limits on the adaptations of which the unitary state is capable. This consideration is particularly relevant in cases where there is a conflict of rationalities, such as that in the Americas between the order of the nation-state and that of the Indian peoples. The Indian communities have values and projects that cannot find a place in the frameworks inherited from the West.[80] Similar conflicts could in part account for the failure of nation-building endeavours in Africa following decolonization.[81]

To the extent that a compromise is possible, by contrast, its jural implementation underlines the paradox of the minority demand which by proclaiming the rights of a group asks the law of the state for it. The demand for law causes the state to penetrate into areas from which it had previously been absent. It strengthens its grip on society. The rule of law is essential to the organization of liberties in modern societies, but its advances still reduce individuals' sphere of autonomy.[82] This has very real implications in the case of minority groups, first of all from the point of view of the members of the minorities themselves. The fact that they are addressing the state is already a sign of recognition of its centrality and power. But it also indicates a loss of autonomous effectiveness on the part of the minority order: in order to preserve itself, to continue to assume its functions, the minority group needs the help of the state order. By satisfying the demand, the state can thus obtain more in reality than it gives in appearance. It strengthens its centrality, authenticates its role of universal protector and supreme dispenser, and increases among the members of the minorities the feeling of belonging to the nation-state.[83]

As a rule, the state does not endorse rights without regulating the exercise of them, and does not recognize a social entity without controlling or at least supervising its functioning. For example, the teaching of a minority language in state-run schools implies a more or less direct intervention by the state in the selection of teachers, teaching aids, syllabi, orthography when this is not standardized — all things that touch on the image of the group, the representation of its identity, and in the last analysis affect the fashioning of this identity.

It is then possible to look at these phenomena in two ways, as Patrick Williams does on the subject of recent French treatment of Gypsies. On the one hand, it is a step up: at last having a voice, having a dialogue with the authorities, the Gypsies might themselves begin to control their fate. On the other hand,

It is a work of assignation. The Gypsies reveal who they are and they thus offer a hold to the authorities ... At last united and known, they cease to be the society that was elusive because it was dispersed and unknown. Non-Gypsies can then hope to guide gently, and with a clear conscience, the life of Gypsies ...[84]

The ambiguity of this demand and its acceptance by the state cannot by definition be removed. Only actual practice, which reveals the intention and determination of the protagonists, can reduce it, but always relatively and temporarily.

The Rights of Minorities in the International Order

If we move from the domestic to the international level, law does not lose its ambivalence as the militants sometimes imagine. Far from it. The unreasoning hopes or the erroneous analyses sometimes placed in or made of international law arise essentially from forgetting that the law of international society is first and foremost the law of states.[85] In this connection, two basic features of the international jural order must be briefly mentioned here.

First, the main and full subjects of contemporary international law are always states. Of course, international organizations, endowed with legal personality, have also been granted the quality of subjects of law in the international order. But they are specialized, limited, secondary subjects. International organizations are created by states and possess only those powers and means that states grant them; they only carry on their autonomous activity in the narrow limits left to them by the balances established between states within them and outside them.

Second, the modern state alone possesses sovereignty. This principle was once again recalled by the International Court of Justice in its opinion on the Western Sahara case. The Court rejected the Moroccan claims, observing that the alleged legal bonds between Morocco and the territories in question were not such as to constitute territorial sovereignty. 'In other words, the Court adheres to the traditional line according to which only a state constructed on the European model can be entitled to sovereignty.'[86] Decolonization carried out on this principle must lead to the formation of nations-states since henceforth, in law at least, the only rule recognized internationally is national rule.

Such an international order produces minorities either because it excludes peoples proceeding from another rationality or rejected from history by the way colonies were carved out, or because within states there emerge majorities, or even minorities, that dominate and rule.[87] Then why should international law be concerned about protecting the rights of minorities? Why should states enter into commitments to reform situations that are an element, sometimes a condition, of their power? Why should a state undertake obligations towards other states to guarantee rights to groups which its own practice oppresses or marginalizes?

The answer to these questions can only be political. Of course there are arguments based on goodwill and morality, but they never take states very far. States only accept obligations in the pursuit of their own interests or under constraint. In the area of the 'protection of minorities' (to use the accepted expression), this cold logic can be seen in both bilateral undertakings and in the signing of multilateral conventions. Each time, therefore, the contradiction at the origin of law must be examined.

Between two states there is always a trade-off. It is always necessary to analyse what relationships of force, military or political, enable one state to secure from another state that it guarantee certain rights to certain of its subjects. This state by the same token obtains a right of oversight, or at all events a title to intervene in favour of the said subjects to ensure respect for commitments entered into. There is obviously a risk of unwarranted interference, or of an exacerbation of tensions, if the parties do not act in good faith. In this game, the minorities risk being only the pretext for a confrontation that goes beyond them.

A general system of protection established in the framework of an international organization minimizes these drawbacks. The precedent of the League of Nations, considered to have been a failure, is commonly invoked to criticize this approach, however wrongly. In fact, from a jural point of view, the system was heterogeneous: it rested on a complex network of particular acts or treaties, the summit of which was the League. But above all, it was vitiated politically, since not all states were members. It was part of the peace settlement imposed by the victors: an element of the political stabilization which they wished to see established in central and eastern Europe, following the territorial changes brought about by the peace treaties. By refusing to accept any obligation, the victors discredited from the outset the idea of the protection of minorities.

As we know, with the United Nations Organization an altogether different approach prevailed: human rights. Based in the Charter on 'the dignity and value of the human person', they are proclaimed in the Universal Declaration of Human Rights adopted by the General Assembly on 10 December 1948, and put into legal form in countless international acts, notably in the two international covenants on human rights which were put up by the General Assembly in 1966 for ratification by states and which came into force in 1976. The UN thus marks a new ideological era. On a universal notion of human dignity, it has achieved an extension of human rights worldwide. Historical products of European culture and politics, these have become an ideological and legal reference point all over the world, a permanent reminder to states and a powerful instrument of action for individuals and groups.[88] These developments must not however be separated from the whole of the legal output of the UN, adopted either as proposals to states or as a guide for its own action, in the area of decolonization, political and legal relations between states, and finally worldwide economic relations (the fight against underdevelopment and the search for a new world economic order).

On the issue of minorities, it was widely felt that the guarantee of human rights and good relations between states constituted adequate general solutions. Thus the United Nations refused to insert an article on minorities in the Universal Declaration of Human Rights, and to extend the 9 December 1948 Convention on the Protection and Punishment of the Crime of Genocide to cover cultural genocide. Granting special rights to members of minorities seemed outmoded, apart from the settlement of a few special cases that were part of the settlement of already internationalized conflicts (the South Tyrol affair, for example). Hence the virtual nonexistence down to the present day of a general international law of minorities. On the other hand, the fight against discrimination in the enjoyment of the rights guaranteed by the Universal Declaration was pursued vigorously and resulted in the adoption of numerous documents which give minorities at least the guarantee of individual equality. Particularly significant by reason of their legal value are the 1965 International Convention on the Elimination of All Forms of Racial Discrimination and the general clause on non-discrimination laid down in article 2 of the two conventions on human rights.[89]

In reality, minority problems have only become more intense and more numerous with the increase in the number of sovereign states. The UN has had to involve itself with them, certainly in a very secondary way, but nevertheless continuously, including legally. A Sub-Commission on Prevention of Discrimination and Protection of Minorities was entrusted with the following task:

> To undertake studies, particularly in the light of the Universal Declaration of Human Rights, and make recommendations to the Commission on Human Rights dealing with the fight against discriminatory measures of all sorts taken in violation of human rights and fundamental freedoms, as well as on the subject of the protection of racial, national, religious and linguistic minorities.[90]

It is in this framework, defined by the Declaration of Human Rights, that the question of minorities as such is dealt with at the UN. The granting of collective or special rights is only contemplated reluctantly and with suspicion as a corrective and preferably transitional measure. Very revealing in this respect is the insistence with which it is stressed that the beneficiaries of these rights are the members of minority groups and not the groups themselves.

Numerous studies have been carried out in the framework of the Sub-Commission into the various forms of discrimination. But most importantly, the work of the Sub-Commission has resulted in the insertion of an article 27, relative to minorities, in the International Covenant on Civil and Political Rights. This stipulates that:

> In those States in which ethnic, religious or linguistic minorities exist, persons belonging to such minorities shall not be denied the right, in community with the other members of their group, to enjoy their own culture, to profess and practise their own religion, or to use their own language.

The weaknesses of this article are obvious. It neither contains a definition of minorities nor makes any provision for a body to designate them: the failure to designate the beneficiaries is alone enough to explain the unanimity of states on this wording. But in addition, the rights recognized are very vague: the clause only imposes on states an obligation to abstain from certain actions. The experts and delegates who participated in its drafting were unanimous, whether they welcomed it or deplored it, on the fact that article 27 was not basically designed to ensure the preservation of minority groups. The Yugoslav delegate, certainly one of the best disposed on this subject, brought out clearly the aim pursued by the international community, saying that:

> The present article did not affect the integrity of the State and should not be allowed to obstruct the process of assimilation of minority groups. But that assimilation must be free and unconstrained. There was a danger that, in order to encourage assimilation, a Government might adopt measures detrimental to the interests of minority groups.[91]

Article 27 is intended to ward off this danger. A modest ambition, but a considerable result — if it were attained.

In pursuit of this aim the Sub-Commission commissioned and secured the publication of a study focused directly on minorities. Carried out by Professor Capotorti, the study recommended that a declaration on the rights of members of minority groups be drafted within the framework of the principles set forth in article 27 of the Covenant.[92] This idea has gained ground and for some years the Sub-Commission has therefore been working, on the basis of a Yugoslav draft, to draft a United Nations Declaration on the 'rights of persons belonging to national, ethnic, religious and linguistic minorities'.[93]

In addition to these UN documents, there have been efforts by the specialized agencies such as the ILO and UNESCO to fight against discriminatory practices in their respective domains. These two international organizations have drafted conventions which, if effectively followed by states, would ensure, directly or indirectly, a degree of protection for minority groups.[94]

Such is the content of general international law on the protection of minorities. To it can be added for the record the regional systems of protection of human rights in Europe, the Americas and Africa, in so far as they benefit minorities by the guarantee of non-discrimination. Finally, we must cite the Helsinki Accords, which are not legally binding but express commitments, at least on the political level. In the Final Act, the states state that they will generally 'respect human rights and fundamental freedoms, including the freedom of thought, conscience, religion or belief, for all without distinction as to race, sex, language or religion'. One particular provision aims at minorities in the following terms:

> The participating States on whose territory national minorities exist will respect the right of persons belonging to such minorities to equality before the law, will afford them the full opportunity of the actual enjoyment of human rights and fundamental freedoms and will, in this manner, protect their legitimate interests in this sphere.

The convergence of the various documents cited is striking, both in their inspiration and in their wording. In the many organizations in which they meet, states are thus always pursuing the same goal. The ideal declared, and no doubt often sought, is to satisfy the profound aspirations of humanity. The goal pursued is more concrete: the stabilization of the international order. It is a matter of affirming and if possible securing respect for shared values, but also at the same time of confirming the model of the sovereign state as the framework of political domination by promoting to that end the formation of national societies.

The UN system is the particular chosen place where a complex interplay of political and ideological pressures is put on states to move them closer to these aims. Non-governmental organizations play an important and increasing part in this interplay. Their claim to defend universal values and their successes now tend to make them the appointed spokesmen of international opinion and the repositories of a new legitimacy competing insidiously with that of states.

Looked at from this political standpoint, the protection of minorities through the guarantee of human rights and the passive tolerance of differences appears to be less a humanitarian pressure than a condition for the good functioning of international society. Political and jural discourses sketch out the outlines of the model state. They provide points of reference, advice and admonishments for the building of a modern, well-managed national society. The oppression of minorities is contrary to the official values of the world order, a source of domestic and international tensions, and finally an impediment to development. The protection of minorities, to take the obverse, relaxes tensions and makes possible the identification of populations with their state. In the words of Capotorti,

> Experience shows that in a society where several cultures coexist, the most effective way of building a just, peaceful and united nation, consists for the state concerned in adopting a policy enabling the members of ethnic, religious and linguistic minorities to maintain their own peculiar characteristics.[95]

In the final analysis, international law simply refers back to the ambivalence of the protection of minorities in domestic law.

Conclusion

The jural approach described in this chapter might encourage a feeling of powerlessness. It shows the close relationship between the social order and the jural order, the constraints of the jural order built on a rationality that is necessarily unique, the subordination or infiltration by the state order of other orders, the logical link that unites national orders and international order in general interaction. Law simply requires rigour: it encourages realism but not inaction. The notions of jural order and relevance bring out the variety of possible settlements of the minority situation. But they also show that the minority question is central in contemporary political disputes since it raises the question of legitimacy.

Notes

1. On these questions see P.-J. Simon, 'Propositions pour un lexique des mots clés dans le domaine des études relationelles', *Pluriel-débat*, 1975, no. 4, p. 65 et seq.
2. Alex Weill and François Terré, *Droit — introduction générale*, 4th edition, Paris, Dalloz, 1979, pp. 4 and 5.
3. Cf. Danièle Loschak, 'Droit, normalité et normalisation', in *Le droit en procès*, Paris, PUF, 1983, p. 53.

4. Cf. the definition given by M. Alliot: 'Law is both struggle and the consensus on the results of the struggle in the areas that a society holds to be vital.' 'When one lives in society, the individual or collective spheres of action can only be lastingly defended or enlarged to the extent that they are recognized, that is to the extent that there is a consensus to justify or obscure the antagonistic practices from which they result.' In *Bulletin de liaison de l'équipe de recherche en anthropologie juridique* (University of Paris I), no. 6, January 1983, pp. 83 and 85.

5. Jacques Chevallier, 'L'ordre juridique', in *Le droit en procès*, p. 15.

6. Cf. André-Jean Arnaud, 'Critique de la raison juridique', vol. 1, *Où va la sociologie du droit?* , Paris, LGDJ, 1981, p. 359 et seq.: 'Le dire-droit, choix stratégique.'

7. This comment made by André Hauriou about political institutions can be extended to law as a whole: 'Recherches sur une problématique et une méthodologie applicables à l'analyse des institutions politiques', in *Revue de droit publique*, 1971, no. 2, p. 335.

8. See for example the selected bibliography on the subject of the rights and demands of indigenous peoples, in the *Bulletin de liaison de l'équipe de recherche en anthropologie juridique*, p. 45.

9. Cf. A.-J. Arnaud, 'Critique de la raison juridique', p. 279.

10. D. Loschak, 'Droit, normalité et normalisation', p. 72.

11. Cf. J. Chevallier, 'L'ordre juridique', p. 40.

12. Cf. D. Loschak, 'Droit, normalité et normalisation', p. 72.

13. *L'ordre juridique*, P. Francescakis, Paris, Dalloz, 1975.

14. Carré de Malberg, *Contribution à la théorie générale de l'État*, Paris, Sirey, 1920, new edition by CNRS, vol. 1, p. 157.

15. Ibid., p. 187.

16. Ibid., p. 176.

17. Pierre Legendre, *L'amour du censeur, essai sur l'ordre dogmatique*, Paris, Seuil, 1974, p. 195.

18. Carré de Malberg himself says of his viewpoint that 'the problem of the origin of the state ultimately merges with that of the origin of law' (vol. 1, p. 95). He also observes that 'the organized power of the state results from a certain balance of existing social forces' (vol. 1, p. 198).

19. This enables Santi Romano to suggest that 'doubtless the state limits itself by establishing its jural order; but the fact is that it is always limited, precisely because it is from its origin a jural order' (p. 60).

20. Pierre Legendre, *L'amour du censeur*, p. 195.

21. Carré de Malberg, *Contribution à la théorie generale de l'État*, p. viii.

22. This remark is equally true even of the electoral system: it is well known that, depending on the voting system, a majority of seats in parliament can be held by a minority of votes in the electorate.

23. Colette Guillaumin, *L'idéologie raciste, genèse et langage actuel*, Paris and The Hague, Mouton, 1972, p. 221.

24. Francesco Capotorti, *Study on the Rights of Persons Belonging to Ethnic, Religious and Linguistic Minorities*, United Nations, Sub-Commission on Prevention of Discrimination and Protection of Minorities, 22 June 1977. E/CN.4/Sub.2/384/Rev. 1, p. 38. (The significance of this study is brought out below in the discussion of the rights of minorities in the international order.)

It is to this extent that it is possible indeed to say with Sartre that it is the anti-Semite who makes the Jew (*Portrait of the Anti-Semite*, tr. E. de Mauny, London, Secker and Warburg, 1948); in the same way, it is the White man who created the Negro, and the Indian is defined by the non-Indian (on this latter case, cf. Yvon Le Bot, 'Revendications d'identité ou luttes de libération? Problème national en Amérique dite latine', in *Pluriel-débat*, no. 33–4, p. 137); and the Gypsy is defined by the non-Gypsy (cf. P. Williams, 'Les Tsiganes', in *Combat pour la diaspora*, cercle Gaston-Crémieux, no. 11–12, 1983, Paris, Syros, p. 147).

25.   Maxime Rodinson, 'Racisme et Ethnisme', in *Pluriel-débat*, no. 3, 1975, p. 24.

26.   On the Burakumin, see J.-F. Sabouret, *L'autre Japon: les Burakumin*, Paris, La Découverte, 1983.

27.   F. Capotorti, *Study on the Rights of Persons*, p. 8. He proposes the following definition formulated with a view to the implementation of article 27 of the International Covenant on Civil and Political Rights, the article on the rights of minorities cited below:

> A group numerically inferior to the rest of the population of a State, in a non-dominant position, whose members — being nationals of the State — possess ethnic, religious or linguistic characteristics differing from those of the rest of the population and show, if only implicitly, a sense of solidarity, directed towards preserving their culture, traditions, religion or language (para. 568).

28.   R. Marienstras, 'Les juifs ou la vocation minoritaire', in *Les Temps Modernes*, no. 8–9, 1973, p. 489. To this image of the Jew, the West has added that of the Gypsy: cf. J.-P. Liégeois, *Comment peut-on être tsigane?*, Groupement pour les droits des minorités, 1981.

29.   For a more detailed analysis of these points, see A. Fenet, 'La question des minorités — propos sur la souveraineté', in *Realités du droit international contemporain*. Actes des seconde et troisiéme rencontres de Reims, 1975, Faculté de droit de Reims.

30.   On this point, see J. Y. Guyomar, *L'idéologie nationale. Nation, représentation, propriété*, Paris, Champ libre, 1974.

31.   This is well brought out by B. C. Shafer, *Nationalism, Myth and Reality*, New York, Harcourt Brace and World, 1955. See also Alain Fenet, *Essai sur la notion de minorité nationale*, Publications de la Faculté de droit d'Amiens, no. 7, 1977.

32.   On this much discussed point, see for example, René Gallissot, 'Mais qu'est-ce qu'une nation?', in *Pluriel-débat*, no. 1, 1975, p. 7. It should be particularly noted that 'without excessively forcing the words', Stalin's famous definition of the nation could be applied to the whole chain of collectivities of social reproduction.

33.   Carré de Malberg, *Contribution à la théorie générale de l'État*, vol. 1, p. 3.

34.   Language appears so important to many authors that they see in it the criterion of the nation. For some, it is even the core of any nation-building enterprise; cf. Benedict Anderson, *Imagined Communities*, London, Verso/New Left Books, 1983.

35.   J.-P. Chrétien has described this process at work in the African context in the chronicle 'L'alibi ethnique dans les politiques africaines', in *Esprit*, 7–8, 1981, p. 109.

36. See the examples cited by J.-P Chrétien, ibid., pp. 110–11.
37. Guy Héraud, 'Notion de minorité linguistique', in *Minorités linguistiques et interventions. Essai de typologie*, Les Presses de l'Université Laval, Travaux du CIRB, Quebec, 1978, p. 18.
38. Cf. the criticism made by Jean Poirier, op. cit. in note 37, p. 39. It should particularly be stressed that while language is a basic factor of identity, it would be contrary to reality to endow it with an exclusive impact in the political and legal domains. In politics, this has been analysed by numerous authors (cf. particularly B. C. Shafer, *Nationalism, Myth and Reality*). In the legal domain, it is interesting to learn that Swiss researchers have shown the lack of coincidence of customs and languages in Switzerland (*Le Monde*, 10 December 1982, reporting a colloquium held at Aix-en-Provence on the ethnological cartography of Europe).
39. P.-J. Simon, 'Propositions', p. 71. For an overall, and original, discussion of the question of ethnicity, see Danielle Juteau-Lee, 'La production de l'ethnicité or la part réelle de l'idéel', in *Sociologie et sociétés*, Presses de l'Université de Montreal, vol. XV, 2, p. 39.
40. Cf. Camille Scalabrino, 'Nation et reproduction sociale', in *Pluriel-débat*, no. 3, 1975, p. 77.
41. 'Qu'est-ce qu'un peuple?', in *Pluriel-débat*, no. 13, 1976, p. 5.
42. Marianne B. Wilhelm, 'Les minorités sont-elles menacées d'ethnocide?', in *Droits de l'homme et droits des peuples*, Republic of San Marino, 1983, p. 205.
43. Cf. Richard Marienstras: 'And action for this survival begins where one lives, where one works, where one is. There is no identity maintained by proxy, any more than one can do politics by proxy. That implies not only an effective self-management of community bodies, but the conviction that the community to which one belongs is lasting, necessary, and morally and culturally worthy of respect, devotion and sacrifice', in *Combat pour la diaspora*, p. 130.
44. Capotorti, *Study on the Rights of Persons*, para. 571.
45. R. Marienstras in *Combat pour la diaspora*, p. 124.
46. Cf. *La France au pluriel*, L'Harmattan, 1984. This book contains the proceedings of a colloquium at Amiens in December 1982, organized jointly by the Centre de Relations Internationales et de Sciences Politiques d'Amiens and the journal *Pluriel-débat*, on the theme 'La France au pluriel?'
47. On this point see the analyses of Corsica by Wanda Dressler-Holohan, in *Pluriel-débat*, no. 32–3, 'Itinéraire d'une recherche sur les mouvements sociaux nationalitaires en France', p. 39.
48. R. Marienstras in *Combat pour la diaspora*, p. 123.
49. A theory of solidarity, from which I borrow in part, is put forward by Michael Hechter in *Pluriel-débat*, no. 32–3, p. 126.
50. Cf. Mr Theo Klein, President of the Representative Council of Jewish Institutions in France: 'the community as such, as an institution …', in *Le Monde*, 23 March 1984.
51. Still using the same example of the Jewish community, cf. Rabbi Sirat, Grand Rabbi of France: 'Now, Judaism stands as it has for millennia and as it should never have ceased to be, that is as a global system that cannot be restricted to its strictly liturgical dimension', *Le Monde*, 13 August 1982.

    To take the example of an apparently linguistic community: in Belgian Flanders, 'A priest is worth twenty policemen', it used to be said, according to Maurice T. Maschino, 'La Belgique en voie de pacification', in *Le Monde Diplomatique*, July 1978.

52.   'Où en est l'occitanisme?', in *Pluriel-débat*, no. 26, 1981, p. 68.

53.   On the subject of 'the ever conflictual nature of an ethnic group', Denise Helly observes generally that 'relationships of force internal to any ethnic group are the source of a particular hierarchy, a leadership and a specific formulation of its past and identity. They also generate other definitions of this implicit past and identity, unvoiced by the socio-economic categories that have been subordinated in the group.' 'Mouvements nationalitaires en République populaire de Chine: le cas des musulmans au Xinjiang, 1949–1963', in *Pluriel-débat*, no. 32–3, p. 97. Many features make it possible to apply her conclusion to the French case: 'It seems that in the industrialized countries nationalitarian demands are rooted in the development of "ethnic bureaucracies" promoted by the growth of the public service sector. This development implies a challenge to the hierarchy and leadership internal to the different groups concerned whereas in fact the situation of exclusion of these latter has not been abolished but is simply taking on new forms' (ibid., p. 98).

54.   The Gypsies appear to be an exception in this respect given that among them there is no centre. The reason for this is that the encounter, and exchange through nomadism, constitute the very definition of the group. Their nomadism in fact must be seen 'not as an endless moving about, but as an occasion for encounters that are forever being repeated'. 'The multiplication of these encounters is what forms the basis of the community.' Patrick Williams, 'Les Tsiganes', pp. 149 and 152.

55.   Here we are thinking of the Basque country, South Tyrol, or the many minorities in central Europe until the period of the population transfers of the twentieth century.

56.   A.-J. Arnaud shows for example that gaming debts, not recognized in French law, derive neither from morality nor custom, but in fact from the jural. 'Critique de la raison juridique', p. 281.

57.   Cf. A.-J. Arnaud, ibid, pp. 20–6; criticized by J. Chevallier, in *L'ordre juridique*, p. 13.

      The importance of this distinction lies in reminding us of the will and capacity of the state to impose its law: 'By definition, an imposed law does not tolerate being gainsaid.'

58.   On the law of the 'milieu', cf. A.-J. Arnaud, 'Critique de la raison juridique', p. 283.

59.   Santi Romano, op. cit., p. 99.

60.   Cf. A.-J. Arnaud:

> In the same way, are the various women's liberation movements aiming at securing changes in the required roles? Do they seek a precise status? On the whole, they are very careful not to make any such demand, conscious as they are of the fact that a status encloses its holder, that the establishment of a status supposes the recognition of an authority which grants it, and that the characteristic feature of a status lies in differentiating what women, precisely, reject. And that is in part why the movement, despite an undeniable social impact, is very muddled jurally. Women are divided on the desirability of having the courts and even the legislature intervene in their cause. This is because the heart of the problem lies elsewhere ('Critique de la raison juridique', p. 292).

Things are different among American feminists. Bella Abzug, a leading figure in the feminist movement, analyses the specific domination suffered by American women and draws the following conclusions: 'We must assert ourselves as an independent political force... We are not going to sit by and let others organize us' (*Le Monde Dimanche*, 17 October 1982).

61.   This observation is particularly applicable to the case of France and the situation of minority languages there. 'In strict doctrinal orthodoxy, French democracy harbours no hostility towards alien languages. It wishes them neither life nor death: it ignores them.' Guy Héraud, *Peuples et langues d'Europe*, Paris, Denoël, 1966, p. 193. That is why Carré de Malberg can argue that France rests on 'the shared national feeling of all parts of the population' and that the system of French public law 'has drawn from that precious qualities of sincerity, uprightness, and consequently, clearness and clarity' (op. cit, vol. 1, p. 63).

62.   Santi Romano, op. cit., p. 90.

63.   Capotorti, *Study on the Rights of Persons*, rev. 1, para. 313. See also C. Coulon, 'Idéologie jacobine, État et ethnocide', in *Pluriel-débat*, no. 17, 1979.

64.   It is worth recalling here the historical reality of linguistic oppression in France. Cf. sub-prefect Romieu, during the July Monarchy: 'Let us create for the improvement of the Breton race some of those prizes that we reserve for horses, and let us make the clergy back us by giving first communion only to children who speak French' (quoted by Yves Person, in *Critique socialiste*, no. 11, p. 48).

65.   Cf. Hans Zorn: 'Whether it is to do with the functioning of our schools, the teaching of our language, the upkeep of our natural and cultural heritage..., the local councils can do both much and little. Of course they are closely watched over by the prefecture and short of resources. But they still hold a small piece of our autonomy' (*Rot und Wiss*, no. 30, 1978, Strasbourg). These observations, made even more pertinent by the decentralization laws, drew on the lessons of the so-called Breitenbach affair precipitated by the decision of the mayor and municipal council of this Alsacian commune to replace the old Alemanic names of streets and places by ordinary French names.

66.   Cf. C. Guillaumin, *L'idéologiste raciste*, p. 204. Compare this comment by a woman participant in the 1982 Amiens colloquium on cultural diversity in France: 'The question is less knowing what one is than having the autonomous power to say oneself what one is.'

67.   In this respect, it may be thought for example that the tens of thousands of people who demonstrated several times in the spring of 1984 in favour of private (i.e. Catholic) education in many towns in Brittany is better testimony to the present identity of Brittany than the small group of marchers who came to Paris at about the same time to plead with the Élysée in favour of the so-called 'Diwann schools', bilingual schools (*Le Monde*, 15 May 1984, 'Les écoles Diwann veulent devenir publiques').

68.   On this question in the North American context, see Raymond Breton, 'La communauté ethnique, communauté politique', in *Sociologie et sociétés*, vol. XV, 2, 1984, p. 23.

69.   Conversely, an attempt to create a community on the basis of 'pied-noir' (former White French settlers in Algeria who had settled in France after independence) Algerianism was abortive. Cf. Albert Bensoussan, 'Les rapatriés d'Algérie: une minorité sans territoire?', in *Pluriel-débat*, no. 25, 1981, p. 41.

Nationalitarian is a rendering of the expression 'nationalitaire' coined some years ago by Anouar Abdel-Malek, and should not be confused with 'nationalist'.

70.   Cf. J. Berque, *Pluriel-débat*, no. 13, 1978, p. 14.
71.   Cf. H. Giordan, *Pluriel-débat*, no. 10, 1977, p. 88.
72.   Cf. R. Gallissot, *Pluriel-débat*, no. 6, 1976, p. 8.
73.   This is the conclusion Wanda Dressler-Holohan reaches about Corsica. 'I now see,' she says,

> the Corsican national movement as the global and many-sided response by certain fractions of a dependent society to the rearrangement of its relationships with the centre that disrupts them, upsets their balances of social reproduction and attempts to impose on them a mode of development that they reject... But while being a powerful tool of mobilization of the forces for autonomy and resistance to domination, this demand makes it too easy for the hegemonic powers, whoever they be, to manipulate symbols, if it only rests on an identity ideologically reconstructed by social forces aspiring to hegemony, without a real popular base of support or a solid revolutionary political content; as seems to be the case in societies that are too unstructured, too dependent or too divided like Corsica ('Itinéraire d'une recherche sur les mouvements sociaux nationalitaires en France', in *Pluriel-débat*, no. 32-3, 1983, pp. 44 and 51).

A participant in the debates at the above-mentioned 1982 Amiens Colloquium commented that the Corsican drift into nationalism was simply following the Corsican drift into the French state, now that the latter has proved impossible.
The paralysis of the Corsican regional assembly has confirmed these political analyses at the institutional level.
74.   This is exactly the content of the manifesto accompanying the 'first march for equality and against racism' from Marseilles to Paris in the autumn of 1983. 'Equal rights and equal opportunities,' it claimed, 'in a plural and solidary nation.' 'What Toumi [a young Maghribi wounded by a police bullet] wanted to demand among other things, was equality in the right to life, equality in the right to respect, equality in the right to happiness here in France...'
75.   On the subject of the struggle waged by the Indian peoples of Latin America, Yvon Le Bot observes that 'the creation of Indian republics on the Bantustan model or on the model of that of the colony would not abolish racism. Sometimes put forward by governments, parties or international bodies, it does not moreover correspond to the demands by autonomous Indian organizations' (op. cit., p. 148).
76.   Santi Romano, pp. 106, 107.
77.   Cf. A.-J. Arnaud, 'Critique de la raison juridique' especially the second part of the work.
78.   Ibid., p. 27.
79.   Ibid., p. 361.
80.   Cf. Dave Akenaken, a delegate to the World Assembly of Primary Nations held at Regina, Canada, in July 1982: 'We have informed governments that we want to control our own lives, our own economic development, our own education, our own health services, our own housing programmes... We want to exercise our right as human beings to self-determination', in *Bulletin Amérique indienne*, no. 20, 1980.
81.   Cf. Michel Alliot: 'African societies thus obey a plural logic which is the opposite, it seems, of that of most European societies... In such societies, legislation that aims at uniformity is felt as destructive of unity, and the state,

when it has existed potentially in memory and expectation or even in fact, never attempted to impose such legislation before conceiving itself on the European model. It was concerned with the greatness of the people, but the unity of the people was the responsibility of all' ('L'anthropologie juridique et le droit des manuels', in *Bulletin de liaison de l'équipe de recherche en anthropologie juridique*, no. 6, 1983). For a systematic comparative study, see Étienne Le Roy, 'L'introduction du modèle de l'État européen en Afrique francophone — logiques et mythologiques du discours juridique', paper presented to the theoretical seminar, Connaissance du Tiers Monde, 1982.

82. Cf. W. Leisner: 'The rule of law is in the last analysis the enemy of the autonomies that can never be perfectly watched. Legality is centralizing, it increases the powers of the state, it integrates them into the unity of the norm-state, thus producing the unity of power, power *tout court*' (cited by J. Chevallier and D. Loschak, *Science administrative*, Paris, LGDJ, 1978, vol. 1, p. 521).

83. Cf. B. C. Shafer: '... it followed that as men appealed to and received benefits from the nation, they tended to identify themselves with it and with the state that symbolized it' (*Nationalism. Myth and Reality*, p. 159).

84. Patrick Williams, 'Les Tsiganes', pp. 155–6.

85. By way of example, this headline concerning 'Breton nationality recognized by the UN' announced quite seriously that 'by the terms of a joint decision of the Office of the United Nations, UNICEF, UNESCO, the European Court of Human Rights and the International Court at the Hague, the children of Jean-Jacques le Goarnic are henceforth European citizens of Breton Nationality' (article in *L'Avenir de la Bretagne* of 22 February 1975, reprinted in *Embata* of 6 March 1975). No comment is necessary.

86. Jean Salmon, 'Droits des peuples et droits des États', in *Réalités du droit international contemporain*, Faculté de droit de Reims, 1976, p. 221.

87. Once again we shall use the example of the Indians to illustrate the concept of a demand that cannot be integrated into the established order; Sol Anderson, an Indian delegate to the Regina World Assembly of Primary Nations mentioned above: 'We want the right to coexist as nations with those that share our lands. That is what we mean by self-determination... By holding this assembly, we want to make it known to all those nations that make up the United Nations that we are knocking at the door and that we want to come in' (in *Bulletin Amérique indienne*, no. 20, October 1982). It will be a long time before the door opens...

88. This worldwide spread has received a new endorsement in the adoption in the framework of the OAU of an 'African Charter of the Human and People's Rights' (Nairobi, 28 January 1981), and the proclamation of a 'Universal Islamic Declaration of Human Rights' (Paris, 19 September 1981). These documents are published with an introduction by Alain Fenet *et al.*, *Droits de l'homme — droits des peuples*, Paris, PUF, 1982.

89. a) Article 1 of the 1965 Convention:

> 1. In this Convention, the term 'racial discrimination' shall mean any distinction, exclusion, restriction or preference based on race, colour, descent, or national or ethnic origin which has the purpose or effect of nullifying or impairing the recognition, enjoyment or exercise, on an equal footing, of human rights and fundamental freedoms in the political, economic, social, cultural or any other field of public life.

2. This Convention shall not apply to distinctions, exclusions, restrictions or preferences made by a State Party to this Convention between citizens and non-citizens.

3. Nothing in this Convention may be interpreted as affecting in any way the legal provisions of States Parties concerning nationality, citizenship or naturalization, provided that such provisions do not discriminate against any particular nationality.

4. Special measures taken for the sole purpose of securing adequate advancement of certain racial or ethnic groups or individuals requiring such protection as may be necessary in order to ensure such groups or individuals equal enjoyment or exercise of human rights and fundamental freedoms shall not be deemed racial discrimination, provided, however, that such measures do not, as a consequence, lead to the maintenance of separate rights for different racial groups and that they shall not be continued after the objectives for which they were taken have been achieved.

b) Article 2 of the 1965 Covenant on Civil and Political Rights:

1. Each State Party to the present Covenant undertakes to respect and to ensure to all individuals within its territory and subject to its jurisdiction the rights recognized in the present Covenant, without distinction of any kind, such as race, colour, sex, language, religion, political or other opinion, national or social origin, property, birth or other status.

90.   UN, Commission on Human Rights, 5th session, E/1371, p. 13.
91.   UN, General Assembly, 3rd Committee, A/C.3/SR. 1104.
92.   Study on the Rights of Persons Belonging to Ethnic, Religious and Linguistic Minorities, E/CN.4/Sub. 2/384, Rev. 1.
93.   Cf. Alain Fenet, 'Le projet de Déclaration des Nations Unies sur les droits des minorités', in Cao Huy Thuan *et al.*, *Actualité de la question nationale*, Paris, PUF, 1980; text of the Yugoslav proposal, p. 200.
94.   ILO resolutions include the 1938 resolution concerning the renunciation of discrimination which might affect workers belonging to certain races or confessions; convention no. 107, Indigenous and Tribal Populations Convention 1957; convention no. 111, Discrimination (Employment and Occupation) Convention 1958; recommendation no. 111, Discrimination (Employment and Occupation) Recommendation, 1958.

UNESCO's Convention Against Discrimination in Education was adopted by the General Conference on 14 December 1960 and came into force in 1962. Article 5 contains special provisions for minorities:

1. The states parties to this convention agree that:
... (c) It is essential to recognize the right of members of national minorities to carry on their own educational activities, including the maintenance of schools and, depending on the educational policy of each state, the use or the teaching of their own language, provided however:
(i) That this right is not exercised in a manner which prevents the members of these minorities from understanding the culture and language of the community as a whole and from participating in its activities, or which prejudices national sovereignty;
(ii) That the standard of education is not lower than the general standard

laid down or approved by the competent authorities; and
(iii) That attendance at such schools is optional.

UNESCO's activity is especially important for minorities in so far as this organization places special emphasis on the promotion of cultural identity. The current five-year plan aims specifically at the promotion of cultural identity as a factor of independence and solidarity and of mutual appreciation between individuals, groups, nations and regions, as well as at the promotion of respect for the cultural identity of individuals and groups, in particular of those suffering marginalization in developed or developing societies.

95.   Capotorti, *Study of the Rights of Persons,* V. p. 13.

Part I

3

The Notion of Minority
and Islam

MAXIME RODINSON

The conception of minority communities as groups whose members must be guaranteed the same rights as the majority and which are entitled to a collective existence is an idea which only began to be publicly recognized in 1919. It is not surprising, therefore, that this notion of equal rights does not appear in the classical Muslim doctrine developed in the high Middle Ages.

Hierarchical Pluralism

On both a practical and theoretical level, by contrast, the recognition of the existence of subordinate communities within a state is universal. In this structure, each minority group enjoys a particular status, involving both submission and acceptance (and hence a degree of protection). In Islam this takes on special features. Here as elsewhere, communities declared to be illegitimate are excluded from these arrangements.

In the past as today, 'legitimate' minority communities were treated as inferior, subordinated, in one way or another, but were not necessarily minorities. Democratic ideology has led people to confuse the two concepts: no one should be treated as inferior, but if some are, they are then a minority. People speak of minorities, therefore, whenever there is inferiority. But those who have thought about the issue are aware that this manner of seeing things is inadequate. 'There is a wide consensus among sociologists that the term [minority group] should not be regarded as a statistical concept,' writes the American sociologist Preston Valien in the *Dictionary of the Social Sciences* published under the auspices of UNESCO.[1] In other words, a 'minority group' may very well be the majority in a given country.

In the classical Muslim world, the demand for the ideal state of truth was proclaimed and people adapted to the rule of the actual existing state based on force. In the beginning, the two were deemed to coincide: the state of force was seen, at least potentially, as the state of truth. Later a few nuances were added, and the gap between the two concepts was clearly recognized. The most radical, those who saw not a gap but a gulf, attempted to make the two one again by using, precisely, force. And so it still is today.

In these two images, there is no question of the rights of the minority or of the majority. The state of force gives power to the strongest. The state of truth legitimizes the power of those who hold the truth. Weakness does not have the strength to prevail over force. Error has no right to prevail over truth.[2] Numbers count for nothing.[3]

In passing, we should note the theoretical difference from Christian conceptions, for this theoretical gap had and has practical consequences. The doctrine of Islam presupposes a state of truth. Christian doctrine, for historical reasons, recognizes only a community of truth which must secure the support of the state of force, but never identify itself with it.

There are two types of 'minority' community in the conventional sense that is, that do not have a sense of belonging to the community that provides the political powerholders and/or proclaims a truth that it has the power to impose.

There are ethnic 'minorities'. These are 'sub-groups within a culture which are distinguished from the dominant group by reason of differences in physiognomy, language, customs or cultural patterns (including any combination of these factors).' 'Such sub-groups are regarded as inherently different and "not belonging" to the dominant group; for this reason they are consciously or unconsciously excluded from full participation in the life of the culture,' adds the American sociologist R. A. Schermerhorn, who suggests this definition.[4] First and foremost, in the cases we are concerned with here, they are communities that claim allegiance to an identity that is of a different origin from that of the dominant group; they thus bear the name of a different people and usually speak a different language.

They must be distinguished in part from religious or confessional 'minorities' that are simply confessions. They are distinguished from the dominant group in principle by their ideas and ideology and by the practices that these ideas call for. Practically speaking, for the periods and the region we are concerned with, religious ideas and rites helped group these minorities into structured communities that in many ways resembled small nations, or quasi-nations.[5]

In the classical Muslim world, 'ethnic minorities' were not normally taken into account. People could identify themselves as belonging to one or other of them, as Arabs, Persians, Turks, Berbers, etc. But this identification was of little or no social relevance compared to the identification by life-style (nomads, settled peasants, city-dwellers) or in relation to religious communities. It should be noted that the situation was virtually the same in the Christian world of the West in the Middle Ages. People identified themselves as Christians before seeing themselves as Frenchmen (or Poitevins, Burgundians, Picards, etc.), Spaniards (or Castillians, Aragonese, etc.), Italians (or Tuscans, Lombards, etc.).

In the same world there were thus 'minority' confessions; this was the essential difference recognized by public law and consciousness among the subjects of the same state. They were normally subordinate, since in practice they were the weakest and in theory they were not the community of truth, at least not of the whole truth. This may be described as a hierarchical pluralism. Among them were some minorities seen as legitimate ones and for whose treatment the term 'tolerated' is not altogether adequate. They enjoyed a well defined, codified status, involving submission and protection. These were the ones that, in theory (according to the definition of the dominant groups), were monotheists: Christians, Jews, Zoroastrians. There were also illegitimate ones that might sometimes be tolerated in practice, but which had, in theory, to be driven out or eradicated, since they represented a criminal lie, a blasphemy, a prejudice against God. These were the 'idolatrous' polytheists.

Relations between the members of the various ethnic groups (one can scarcely talk of 'communities') were not codified since they were often not noticed; their affiliations were often not clear, the importance attached to them being much less significant, as we have seen, than the groups' attachment to a given life-style, confession or social stratum (the elite and the mass according to the usual categorization in the Islamic Middle Ages). There were, of course, exceptions: people of Arab stock in the first century of the Hegira were politically privileged, so were the Turks in the Mamluk states, etc. But neither the subjects nor the theoreticians normally found it scandalous that a mass belonging to one ethnic group was ruled by a monarch and a class of leaders belonging to another ethnic group. Indignation on this subject is a recent development in the world of Islam.

On the other hand, the status of the subordinate legitimate confessions was strictly defined by Muslim canon law. This was the well-known status of *dhimma*, that is, of protection granted by a superior to an inferior. It was the rule for the members of the monotheistic confessions. Under this system, the protected person enjoyed security in his person and his goods, and the community followed its own rules and administered itself autonomously under the authority and responsibility of leaders recognized and respected by the government. At the same time, the individual had to be subject to the general rules of the state, pay a special tax, not show 'insolence' towards the dominant confession, bear the external marks of recognition of his status as a 'protected person' (*dhimmi*) and non-member of the dominant community, and not proselytize among members of the dominant group.[6] In many respects these restrictions are similar to those imposed on members of churches and other confessional bodies in the USSR and Soviet-dominated countries. They have — in theory — the right to freedom of conscience and worship. But only the freedom of anti-religious propaganda is recognized (article 52 of the 1977 constitution).[7] The privilege of superiority due to the possession of the truth is thus recognized for a 'confession' that is deviant by comparison with medieval conditions: the 'confession' of the atheists.

The system thus organized reached its highest point of codification in the Ottoman empire. That is why it is often designated by the Turkish term as the system of *millets*. *Millet* is the Turkified form of the Arabic word *milla(t)*, plural *milal*. The term has, as usual, had a rather wide range of meanings. Equivalents might be: nation; religious community; religion, religious doctrine peculiar to a nation, to a community. The organization of each in a relatively autonomous social unit, endowed with both its own administration and a doctrine, is the important point.

Decay and Exploitation of the System

The picture changed during the nineteenth century as the Muslim states weakened. This weakening was accompanied by the influence of the culture of the now preponderant powers, as is sociologically the rule. The ideologies and types of political and social structure developed in Europe over several centuries progressively penetrated the Muslim world from all sides. An important factor in this penetration (when it was not directly imposed by force) was the fact that Western ideology and social structure were seen as the causes of the political, economic, scientific and military superiority acquired by the West, and of its progress, which at the time seemed to be permanent, on the road to wealth and well-being.

Another factor that was having the same effect — and one that was to prove to be more important — was that these ideologies and the structures they inspired were in line with universal human aspirations, present at least potentially in the world of Islam as elsewhere, but repressed for centuries. It was generally accepted, under the impact of economic and political conditions, that they were unachievable. A little later than in Europe, people began to glimpse that they might no longer be unachievable. 'Happiness is a new idea in Europe,' said Saint-Just. In the following century, this idea slowly penetrated into the Muslim world. It was the end of resignation.

Popular attitudes reflected this sea-change as people began to demand participation in all the decisions of government and the suppression of inherited privileges. The elites of the dominant confession took the first steps; they felt themselves authorized by virtue of the new principles to demand a share in the process of political decision-making as well as guarantees for the security of their persons and goods. These guarantees were cruelly lacking under the rule of despotic monarchies, the usual form of government in the Muslim countries. Moreover the members of the minority confessions and the European or American foreigners enjoyed them before the Muslims by virtue of the protection of the dominant powers. These Western powers, whose wishes the local rulers could henceforth scarcely ignore (even if their country was not colonized), expected their nationals (the traders in particular) to enjoy every guarantee in their activities. They also protected the members of the minority confessions who had co-religionists who held power (Christians) or who formed powerful pressure groups (Jews) in their own countries. They were placed to act as intermediaries between the two worlds, a role which they used and from which they benefited.

The elites who demanded a share in power and the governing institutions *vis-à-vis* abuses by the state mobilized the masses to bring pressure to bear to this end and the masses increasingly demanded the same benefits. The framework that best lent itself to these mobilizations was that defined by ethnic membership, although during the transitional period the confessional and multi-ethnic state, both traditional, remained serious rivals of this new nationalist framework. Nationalist ideology — imported from the West but meeting up with deep feelings — exercised a decisive impact. In the Ottoman empire, the Christian communities, Greeks, Serbs, Romanians and Bulgarians had obtained their autonomy and then their independence by virtue of their national characteristics, particularly language. Why then not the Muslim Albanians, Arabs or Kurds? As usual, groups formed around charismatic and ambitious individuals to demand an autonomy or independence that would ensure them power. They embarked on massive mobilizations.

In this process, each of the Western powers, tempted by the weakness of the Muslim states and increasingly adopting everywhere an imperialist policy, found support in one 'minority' community or another. Betting on the divisions in the enemy or the prey being attacked is an eternal law of politics. The leaders of the communities involved were naturally tempted, at the very least, to accept this help. The hierarchical pluralism was exploited by an attempt at external domination.

The members of the 'minority' confessions were faced with a difficult choice. They were divided and oscillated depending on their personal character or situation, and on the varying situations of their country internally and externally. They might aspire to be fully-fledged citizens in a state freed of the direct or indirect domination of the foreigner, in which case they participated in the eventual national struggle for freedom. In return they asked for full freedom and full equality. With the progress of democratic ideas and, to a much lesser degree, practices, the traditional situation of *dhimmi* became intolerable. The full freedom and full equality of all seemed to demand a homogenization of the nation, at least to a very considerable extent. If that path were followed they would end up with the Western type of nation-state.

Among other things, such an evolution presupposed the equal application to all of the legal provisions decreed by the state. But that demanded at least the lowering of the barriers between confessions, the elimination of the special law according to which each one administered itself more or less autonomously. This quasi-autonomy gave excessive powers to the leaders of the community, but it also constituted a certain degree of protection with regard to the decisions of the Muslim state.

The minorities called first for equal treatment of the various confessions, which meant the end of Muslim privileges. The state, as is normal, sought to ensure its hold equally over all its subjects: the confessional barriers were an obstacle to this. There was a certain amount of convergence of interests. But major obstacles soon arose.

The logic of the homogenization of the state implied equal legal rules for all. But each confession, whether the majority one or the minority ones, followed different rules, in theory untouchable because they were sanctioned by a higher law, especially in the area of what is called personal status: family law, marriage law, inheritance law. Special confessional courts were needed to know these rules well and apply them, to have any hope of seeing their decisions respected. Most of the time, no middle solution could be found adaptable to all the legal systems present and the clergy of each confession fiercely defended its positions of control.

It would not of course be possible to follow either logic through to the end, and homogenization could continue only up to a certain point and no further. These limits, however, are hard to fix. The members of the minority confessions were tempted by what is usually called the secular model, applied with most far-reaching effect in France since the separation of church and state. The confessions would be no more than associations of people sharing common ideas — philosophical societies, in short. Their members would in every point obey the legal rules laid down by the state. This is the model that Mustafa Kemal Atatürk wanted to apply. Most Muslim states only adopted it while maintaining the practice of some confessional particularisms.

The minorities soon realized that there was a major drawback in the so-called secular path. In a theoretically homogeneous society, the power of decision-making would belong to the majority or the strongest. In most traditionally Muslim states, the majority was Muslim. The strongest were also usually Muslims.

That would not have been any great problem if the communal structure was wholly reduced to philosophical societies which did not seek to encroach on the domain of the others. But this is not the case in the Muslim world. There was no sharp move from the quasi-nation to the non-community, from one extreme to the other.

The dominant element is always identified as the member of a particular confession. It is always suspected of wanting to take measures that will favour its own confession and oppress the others.

The Muslims, with their previously institutionally guaranteed predominance, but whose traditional beliefs and customs have always been attacked by strangers, suspect in each provision that breaks with Muslim norms a new attack on them. Whenever there appear to be too many former members of minorities in any institution it appears as an act of aggression.

The minorities that wanted to maintain an attenuated 'secularism' and a recognition of the complete equality of confessional groups ran up against one obstacle. If everyone retained his own rules, the Muslim community (or communities) would do the same. Muslim rules had been formulated at a time when it enjoyed undeniable supremacy, and, as was the case in the Christian West in the Middle Ages, the dominant community watched very carefully to ensure that its supremacy would not be challenged in everyday life. A member of the dominant group may not be a servant in the house of a member of a 'minority', for example, and a woman of the dominant community may not marry a 'minority' man. Servant and wife are normally subordinate in these societies and any loss of status, however limited and occasional, was setting a bad example.

In short, the minorities remained attached to a limited pluralism with its hierarchical aspect eliminated. When they advocated homogenization, they meant a homogenization based on the removal of any traces of past Muslim supremacy. As for the Muslims, they saw the only issue as the perpetuation of pluralism, with, at most, some attenuation of the hierarchy or a homogenization that would endorse at least a part of their own norms extended to the whole society. What they do not always see, however, is that these norms are the mark of their past supremacy, in most cases retained thanks to the fact that they are a majority in present-day society.

At the level of the ethnic groups, the penetration of Western nationalist ideology and its associated new democratic spirit gradually mobilized potential demands, and began to make inequalities previously accepted as normal or barely disagreeable in the period of resignation seem unacceptable.

Differentiations at this level became more and more relevant within a single confession, as the boundaries of the ethnic groups became fixed — usually around language. Finally demands began to appear.

The period of struggle against foreign control limited this process for a time. Many saw the 'principal contradiction' in their hostility to this control, which drove them to struggle side by side with members of the dominant ethnic group (and confession). Conversely, others were sensitive to the offers of help from one power or another in its efforts to recruit clients in the region. This was often translated in swings from one position to the other within both the ethnic and confessional minorities.

Contradictions of the Homogeneous State

We shall not attempt here to trace in detail the complex historical process which led to the establishment of national states that were meant to be homogeneous in the area of the world where Islam was dominant; these states were formed on the basis of a desire for autonomous decision-making, in a world context that favoured it and the factors mentioned above.

Yet homogenization bears within it contradictions. These are particularly acute in the world of Islam, but are also manifested elsewhere.

The rule of democracy is that decision-making belongs to the majority. That is accepted quite normally in a homogeneous state. But serious problems arise when there are states within the state.

It would require many nuances to define this concept with any degree of precision and comprehensiveness. Let us say broadly that it refers to every case where a communal formation attributes to itself the role of a global society.[8] In general, no society can tolerate two rival power centres (and even less a large number of them) which both demand the full allegiance of the same individuals and groups. 'Every kingdom divided against itself is laid waste, and no city or house divided against itself will stand,' said Jesus of Nazareth.[9] Nineteen centuries later, as a potential strategist, Lenin echoed him on the impossibility of any lasting dual power.[10]

If it comes to be suspected that the decision of the majority in a theoretically democratic community enables the will of a global group, of a national type, to impose its law on other groups of the same type, one is heading straight for revolt. In this sense, Rousseau was not wrong. Democratic functioning and the willing acceptance of the decisions made by the majority presuppose a high degree of homogenization, and the suppression or elimination of some types of 'intermediate bodies', or at least their reduction to the status of non-political 'philosophical societies'.

The nationalist ideology has conquered all minds here as elsewhere, however camouflaged it may sometimes be. It is normally obsessed with national unity. When it is combined with the adoption of democratic majority rule and the demand for homogeneity which results from it, nationalism has formidable effects.

In the Muslim world, virtually everybody agrees that the confessional and ethnic 'minorities' are an obstacle to the democratic and homogeneous state, for people are aware, even if vaguely, of the incompatibility of democracy and the existence of 'minority' groups of a state type.

This trend seems to signify the elimination of confessional and ethnic particularisms. Yet long ago (and the memory of it is still very much alive), the confessions still had the character of quasi-nations and quasi-states. The logic of political demands means that ethnic minorities are exposed to outbidding by groups that demand for them an autonomous status that makes them virtual states, and in extreme cases, gives them full and complete independence. In either case national unity is threatened.

A larger number of members of the minorities want democracy, but suspect (often rightly) the members of the majority and/or dominant group of using their situation to further their own interests. They are driven to demand homogenization in order to promote the establishment of a democratic state, but paradoxically the pluralist communal structure appears as a protection to them. Unfortunately, communal pluralism always tends to revert to a hierarchy.

The confessional and/or ethnic majority seeks to benefit from the advantages that homogeneous democracy grants the majority. Often it does not even realize that it is thus imposing norms that are sometimes vestiges of Muslim privilege and were the rule in traditional society. It tends to identify itself with the nation and to unify the nation around its own traditional norms.

The fundamentalist movement today is pressing for a return to the old pluralism. But the universal reputation won — including among the masses that it seeks to rouse — by the principles of democracy pushes the movement to adopt the form of democracy. It is in the name of the majority and for its benefit that it will restore the old hierarchical pluralism. In its name, it will pursue every effort by the minority communities to recover, at least partly, their global, quasi-national, character. In its name, it will punish not their lapse from the orthodoxy of government, but their anti-national dealings of the previous period, the least sign of which will be held to indicate a resurgence. It will restore the dominance of the majority community, but by giving it a more national than ideological character, by suppressing the protective barriers that in the Middle Ages mitigated its most extreme effects. The same law of the majority will make it possible *a fortiori* to exclude or eliminate, by police methods, any minority that the doctrine considered previously or makes it possible to consider today as illegitimate.

In short, nationalist ideology, with its obsession with preserving unity, is everywhere put at the service of the preponderance of the previously dominant community, either by trying to restore the old norms governing social life which involve the inferiorization of the minority communities (the fundamentalist version), or by endeavouring to preserve some of the achievements of the nineteenth and twentieth centuries: a tendency to the equal treatment of communities, and the adoption of norms that are more detached from the doctrine of the era of predominance. And all that without prejudice to the more or less democratic character of the regimes on other levels.

Nationalism makes suspect any difference that had or might have political consequences. When fundamentalism is added to it, it gives nationalism the support of a theory and a fervour that are equally intolerant, and susceptible of mobilizing the masses. When the enemy of the national becomes at the same time the enemy of God, the results may be, and are, terrible.

A Few Cases

It might be useful to show in quick outline how these trends have taken concrete shape in various places, especially in rather complicated cases.

Berbers

The people conventionally called Berbers are those inhabitants of North Africa who, while having converted to Islam after the Arab invasion, continued to use the old language of the country, Berber. A large proportion of the rest of the inhabitants are quite simply Arabized Berbers. They are usually called Arabs and not Berbers. One therefore ought to use the word Berber-speakers to describe the first category.

Sometimes Berber-speakers, such as the many in the Moroccan countryside, were given the name Berbers because it is rather similar to 'rustics'. In Algeria, the largest group of them, in the mountains to the east of Algiers, was commonly called 'tribespeople' (*qabâ'ili*, Kabyles). Since the Berber-speakers were among those who had retained the most particularisms, the French colonizers tried to play on them to divide the colonized people. Feeling themselves above all colonized, most refused to play this game. Many played a very important role in the national movement. Often they identified themselves as Arabs. The Arab identification was, in fact, that of most of the population, sanctified as it was both by the historical role of the Arabs as the founders and propagators of Islam and by their present role as representatives of a powerful nationalist and anti-imperialist movement in the East.

That did not mean that they did not recognize their difference from the Arabized elements of the Maghribi population. After independence the relationship between the two identifications took on what might be called a dialectical character. In its natural leaning towards the homogenization of the nation, the state normally chose the Arab identification. It was linked to the prestige of a written language (which was not the case with Berber) and one that was, in addition, sacred, the carrier of a considerable historical heritage and united over a hundred million individuals from the Atlantic Ocean to the Persian Gulf. But every effort by the state to repress and restrict the use of Berber, to downplay the Berber cultural heritage, to inferiorize Berber-speakers who did not know Arabic (and who often knew French, the language of the colonizers) ended up creating or strengthening Berber resistance. This resistance went hand in hand with an exaltation of the Berber past, Berber culture and more or less separatist tendencies. Thus was created in reality what only existed potentially before, a Berber ethnic group. As usual, the demand for the recognition of particularisms and for a degree of decentralization took some groups along the road to autonomism; some reached the point of talking of independence.

Despite the conversion of a small number of Berbers to Christianity, the confessional factor did not arise. They were all Muslims. Yet the Arabic-speaking majority might eventually, if fundamentalism were to triumph, use the pagan, Jewish and Christian past of the Berbers, and their frequent tendency to heresy in the Middle Ages, in the form of opposition to the central government, which has continued to the present, as a weapon against them.

Copts

The case of the Christians of Egypt who are traditionally called Copts is in some respects the opposite of that of the Berbers, although the result is comparable. The Copts are the ancient inhabitants of Egypt who adopted the Arabic language without converting to Islam. The status of *dhimmi* subordinated them, but left them a degree of importance in some roles.

The urban strata were relatively favoured during the process of European political and economic penetration in the nineteenth century. Most were, however, drawn into the wave of Egyptian nationalist struggle against the British protectorate, and then into the current of Arab nationalism where the fact that they spoke Arabic enabled them to be fully integrated.

But the Muslim majority has often taken measures that run counter to their particularisms. The fundamentalist movements, on the other hand, denounce any measures that reduce their medieval condition of *dhimmi*. This denunciation affects the majority Muslim masses, who are concerned to maintain their superiority as true believers. Rulers such as Sadat have thought it clever to attempt to undermine the fundamentalist movement by making concessions on this score. These measures and these attitudes in turn strengthen the Copts in their particularism. They sometimes express this feeling by lambasting 'the Arabs'. So far, the Coptic particularist movement has not taken on a political dimension, and in general Egyptian society militates against such a course. If the fundamentalist-type measures are stepped up, however, one cannot predict that a stronger Coptic movement will not emerge. Another way out is emigration, although this is inconceivable for the mass of Coptic peasants, as it is for most other groups.

Turkey

The charisma of Mustafa Kemal Atatürk, the national hero, drew Turkey — that is the territory with a predominantly Turkish population that remained of the old Ottoman empire — into the path of a Turkish nationalism that sought to be secular. The tendency to homogenization benefited from the expulsion and massacre of significant Greek and Armenian minorities (both ethnic and confessional). But there remains the very large Kurdish ethnic minority (Sunni Muslim) and that of the Alawites which is confessional within Islam (Shi'ite tendency). The violent repression of any Kurdish particularism has been unable to uproot it. On the contrary, its harshness must have turned many Kurds towards separatism, as we shall see below.

Nor has the equally harsh repression in the name of secularism of fundamentalist-type Muslim confessional movements resulted in the abolition of this tendency. Without for the most part daring to go so far as a fundamentalist programme, political parties and movements have been able to use successfully the nostalgia of the ordinary Muslim for the blessed time when Islam was the state religion, and again rulers have sometimes made concessions to this tendency. Here, too, the future may hold some unpleasant surprises for the seculiarists.

The Ba'thists

The Ba'th, the Arab nationalist party of Syrian-Lebanese origin, sought from its very beginnings (from about 1943) to be secular and socialist. Founded by a Muslim and a Christian, it determined in the name of nationalism to remove confessional barriers.

Parties of this type quite naturally attract minorities. Nationalism was the order of the day. Socialism was powerfully attractive. The party was able to recruit many members, notably in Syria and Iraq.

Parties evolve in terms of the social and political situations in which they are historically placed. Their doctrine does not always play the most important role in these evolutions. Usually it shifts and often it is quite simply ignored or contradicted.

The Ba'th came to power in Syria and Iraq largely thanks to its following in the army. In Syria, the army happened to have many officers belonging to the Alawite confession. The majority Sunni bourgeoisie scorned the career of arms and did not want its sons to enlist. Facilities were offered by military academies at the time of the French mandate and later, and the Alawites, for the most part rather poor peasants, sent their children to these relatively cheap schools. A few years later, the graduating classes included many Alawites.

The Alawites or Noçayri-s form one of the numerous branches of the great Shi'ite tendency. Their official doctrine, which has absorbed some pre-Islamic pagan elements from the peasant culture of the region where they lived, has played no role in their social ascent. The Ba'thist groups, carried to power by the pressures of the army or trained as soldiers, were myriad. The group finally in power under the leadership of the winner in the factional struggles, General Hafez Asad, an Alawite, knew that he could count essentially on his relatives, connections, friends in his community. The result in Syria has been a sort of Alawite power in which members of other confessions participate but which the majority Sunnis have every reason to hate. These low-born minority members have seized power from them and it is easy to delve into a large bag of traditional imprecations used against them by the theologians and every leader of classical Islam.

The Syrian Ba'th has moderated somewhat its theoretical secularism, since it is not possible wholly to ignore the communal structures. But it has retained the doctrine, which has contributed to hostility against the party.

In Iraq, events took a different course in a different environment. The Sunnis form the milieu in which leaders have long been recruited. But the so-called twelver Shi'ites (those who have dominated Iran since the sixteenth century) are the majority. Ba'thist power in Iraq has many shortcomings. But it has been able so far to impose a homogenized régime — in the Arab ethnic group at least — in which differences of confessional membership are not taken into account in the mechanism of decision-making. It is remarkable that so few Iraqi Shi'ites should have taken the side of Shi'ite Iran in the current Iraq-Iran war.

Kurds

The Kurds form an ethnic group that is predominantly Muslim. Its members are to be found mainly in Turkey, Iraq and Iran.

Like all other Muslims, Kurds participated in governing in the traditional Muslim states. The position they held in government depended solely on the conditions in which individuals found themselves — their social milieu, their way of life and their regional settlement. There were numerous Kurdish principalities. Kurdish sovereigns ruled easily over states whose population included very few Kurds. As has been explained, ethnic origin was not a relevant factor in classical Islam. Among these rulers, the famous Salâh ed-din, known to Europeans as Saladin, won a reputation as a universally admired Muslim hero. There were many cases of assimilation into other ethnic groups (Turks, Arabs, etc.) and many mixed and doubtful cases.

As with the other ethnic elements, a Kurdish nationalism has recently developed on the basis of existing particularisms. It tends to preserve these particularisms, to sanctify them, to revive them if necessary and to practise a cultural normalization within the ethnic group with a view to mobilizing the group. It demands self-government or independence.

Jews and Israel

The Jews formed one of the confessional communities whose legitimacy was recognized by Muslim law. They thus belonged in the category of *dhimmis*: they had a right to protection and a duty of peaceful acquiescence.

Attitudes towards them varied greatly from place to place and period to period. Though their acceptance could not be questioned, victimization and persecution could be unleashed against them, notably following favours granted by princes to some *dhimmis* (Jewish or Christian) whose co-religionists benefited from them. As in Christendom *vis-à-vis* the Jews, the mass of Muslims reacted to them like 'poor Whites'. Muslims saw their grip on their sole claim to superiority (in this case that of being true believers) threatened and the result was riots to which governments yielded by the strict reapplication of the rules of 'non-insolence' and distinctive marks. They thus paid for the preference they had for the *dhimmis*, very convenient since they were not protected by the structures of 'normal' society, that of the Muslims. After some years, there would be a return to more easy-going practices, but in the meantime treatment was harsh for *dhimmis*, whether Jews or Christians.

In times of persecution or victimization, Muslim persecutors could justify themselves by citing verses from the Koran that were marked by the struggles of the Prophet against the Jews of Medina between AD 622 and 632. The stories, true or false, would be told linking a converted Jew to the formation of this or that Muslim 'heresy'.

From the second half of the nineteenth century in the Middle East (note the limits of time and space), the attitude towards the Jews followed this general pattern. Jews now formed a confessional community whose status evolved towards equality of treatment with the other confessions and towards a reduction of confessional peculiarities. In the Arabic-speaking countries, a number of Arabic-speaking Jews participated in Arab national struggles.

Others took advantage of the facilities offered to the members of minority groups by the fact that they shared religions with subjects of the imperialist powers. They were strengthened (mainly in Egypt) by co-religionists who came from Europe because of the favourable economic conditions. In the Maghrib, where the Jewish communities also enjoyed varying situations, but often suffered like others from the brutality of the ruling classes and the general poverty, the Jews opted decisively for French culture, left their milieu in large numbers, and came to be seen as a privileged group. This was the case particularly in Algeria where the Crémieux decree (1870) gave them French nationality.

Political Zionism (born in 1897) recruited followers in varying numbers depending on local conditions. When this movement succeeded in creating the state of Israel in Arab Palestine in 1948, the feelings of community patriotism that had remained very much alive in the Muslim world led many Jews to sympathize with the new state. In any event, the Arab populations, after Israel's victory over the Arabs and the continuation of cold and hot wars, could not have much sympathy for those who had come out for their enemies. Moreover, the new state repeatedly proclaimed that all Jews throughout the world owed it allegiance. The situation of the Jews in Arab lands — and also in Islamic lands more generally by virtue of Muslim solidarity — became untenable. Most emigrated, not always to Israel.

In Israel itself, the law has retained the structure of communities, hierarchical pluralism, but with the Jewish community being the privileged one. It is the Muslims and Christians who have a status approximating that of the *dhimmis* of the Muslim state in the period of partial homogenization.

Lebanon

In what was to become in 1920 the state called Greater Lebanon, the historical conditions were favourable to the proliferation of confessional communities, Christian, Muslim and others, without the community that held supreme power, Sunni Islam, having the overwhelming majority that it had elsewhere.

This situation has long favoured the intervention of the European powers, relying on one confession or another. Europe obliged the Ottoman empire to grant autonomy to Lebanon (1861) by organizing a sharing of power among the main confessions (1864). The French mandate (1920) continued these provisions (1926 constitution).

In the struggle against the French mandate, the majority of the Lebanese elites agreed on a compromise (1943). The independent state endorsed it. The Muslims, attached to the ideology of unitary Arabism, abandoned this project of a single Arab state in the short term. They adopted the idea of a Lebanese state that they had always been against. The Christians for their part took up Arabism, abandoning the idea of separating themselves from the Arab world, or seeking foreign patronage.

A very strict sharing of functions among the various confessions, extending to all levels of public life, was to be the guarantee against the supremacy of one or other of them. Some privileges were, however, conceded to the Maronite community (one of the Christian confessions of the Catholic faith) in consideration of its supposed numerical predominance at the time of the coming into force of the new statute (1932 census). But economic life was not subject to regulations of this sort and the Christian predominance there was much more striking.

Lebanon thus represents the most complete model of a federation of confessional communities of the classical type. Pluralism was maintained, but the principle of hierarchy was abolished despite the emerging outlines of a new hierarchy. Majority rule was introduced, but was subordinated to the supposed constraints of the maintenance of pluralism. In this situation, each confession, enclosed in its communal patriotism, acted like an independent nation. Each fiercely defended its prerogatives, made coalitions, sought clients within and allies and patrons without. The peaceful and balanced coexistence of confessional quasi-nations was increasingly subjected to pressures that were too strong. Each community had its own policy. In a difficult situation — rivalries between Arab states, the hot or cold war with Israel, efforts by the powers to secure clients and acquire strategic positions — the communities were driven to arm themselves, which Middle Eastern conditions made quite easy. The massive arrival of the Palestinians, especially after their expulsion from Jordan in 1970, seemed to provoke a flagrant imbalance. Forming a group apart, with its own interests, sympathetic to the Muslim communities, it naturally came to adopt the autonomous structure of the confessional communities. The weakness of the Lebanese state and its liberal political structure enabled the Palestinians to wage their fight with Israel out of Lebanon, and to form a real army and a real political entity. Thus Lebanon was exposed to Israeli reprisals.

The fears on the part of some that the opposing coalition was becoming too strong, and the suspicions of all about the actual or supposed encroachments of others led to the terrible civil war which began in 1975 and was exacerbated by outside interference.

Is there a moral? It is that when the confessional communal structure is freed of any institutional control, notably through the supervision of a strong state equipped with the means to enforce respect for the rules it lays down, it can very well, in the right circumstances, end up with the same disastrous results as the anarchic freedom of independent nation-states: war pushed to its furthest limits, to the paroxysm of mutual destruction. It would be wise to remember this moral when people stress what makes them different, when they advocate ever finer carve-ups of a national unity and its state authority.

India

India provides a particularly interesting counter-example to the communal model most common in the Muslim world.

By the eleventh century, the Muslim conquerors had succeeded in establishing their power over most of the Indian subcontinent. But they remained a minority. For a complex range of reasons they were unable or unwilling to convert most of their subjects to Islam.

When the Indian freedom movement to end British rule began to grow, Indian Muslims, who had been dispossessed of most of their political power by the British, found themselves in a situation that was virtually the exact opposite of that of the non-Muslim minorities in the Middle East. They had to make a choice: to join the Indian mass movement, with all the communities together, or to create their own movement which would save them from suffering — after the expected victory — the law of the Hindu majority. The British naturally favoured the second option, which divided and weakened the anticolonialist front.

On the eve of independence (1947), the Muslim movement's choice in favour of autonomy had won a wide militant base in the Muslim community. Many Muslims backed the proposal for the creation of Pakistan, a purely Muslim state in which the Muslims of India would be regrouped. The British gave their stamp of approval to this proposal by suggesting partition of the subcontinent into two states — a division which took place in the midst of terrible massacres.

Yet the majority of the Muslims of India chose to stay in India, a state that declared itself non-confessional and secular and symbolized this choice by selecting a Muslim as (non-executive) head of state.

Just as Muslims elsewhere are suspected of colluding with imperialist foreign powers, so the Muslims of India are suspected of favouring the enemy as soon as a conflict erupts or threatens to erupt with Pakistan. Moreover, India is subject to pressures from Hindu extremism which can also be classified as a fundamentalism. Powerful movements proclaim that the only true India is Hindu India, and express this idea by symbolic provocations. Naturally these tend to alienate Muslims from their loyalty to the Indian state and make them feel unwanted; as a consequence, some look towards Pakistan. Others have sought to prove their allegiance to the Indian homeland by their zeal in the service of India — by, for example, volunteering for dangerous missions during wars against Pakistan. Here again it can be seen that the overlaying of confessional communal structures by those of a theoretically homogenized nation-state inevitably causes serious problems.

Why?

The multiplicity of ethnic groups incorporated into nation-states in modern times, the domination of some over others both in modern times and earlier, the process of ethnic homogenization with all its difficulties and limitations, the nationalist (and even micro-nationalist) reactions in recent times against this homogenization — all this is universal and well known.

The tendency of ideological movements (among which I classify the great monotheistic religions with some reservations) to fissiparity and fragmentation is no less universal, and no less well known.

What is less well known, and more specific to the Muslim world, is the proliferation of legitimate confessions recognized by governments (whatever victimization they may have suffered) and the cohesion which has ensured their survival and their consolidation into quasi-nations and quasi-states.

This is not a universal rule. In the monotheistic religions, particularly in medieval Christianity, the confession in power tended to try to eliminate the confessions that had fallen away from the ruling orthodoxy and those belonging to another religion. By the time of the Reformation, political conditions — after many ups and downs and many bloodbaths — forced the acceptance of a confessional pluralism that was initially hierarchical and then egalitarian. The exception was that of the Jews, a tiny minority tolerated because of the legal heritage of Roman pluralism, theological arguments and practical considerations. Jews were ill-tolerated in many cases and their 'heresies' were before long persecuted pitilessly.

If the world of Islam experienced a different structure in which pluralism was on the whole accepted, that was not due to some innate, intrinsic disposition of Muslims to tolerance or a special philanthropic virtue of Islam, as the admiring Western 'philosophes' of the eighteenth century intimated and as most Muslims (rather naturally) believe, or as today's anticolonialists and third-worldists want to believe (sentimentality counting for more than reason). In fact Muslim pluralism relates to the historical conditions of the birth and early development of Islam. The founder, Mohammed (Mahomet) felt that he was bringing to the Arab people a divine message that was substantially identical to the one that Jews and Christians had received, even if the clerical hierarchies had somewhat distorted and twisted this message. His armed disciples conquered vast territories where the majority of the population was Jewish, Christian or Zoroastrian. The doctrine of the Prophet on the subject of other monotheistic confessions converged with the constraints of the situation. It was impracticable and moreover harmful to the interests of the conquerors to seek the systematic conversion of the faithful of other religions. The pluralist structures of the religions in the world they had conquered, however theoretical they may sometimes have been, offered frameworks to regulate this carefully limited acceptance of rival ideologies. The adherents of these ideologies gradually declined in number as a result of the massive (but not complete) Islamization, to which people were not forced, but which the new social and religious conditions strongly favoured. Nothing could prevent it.

The model of subject and protected legitimate confession offered to the Jews and Christians was extended, for practical reasons, to the Zoroastrians (whose strict monotheism is not altogether obvious), and then, despite the doctrine, to undeniable polytheists as we have seen in the case of India, and finally to a number of Muslim 'heresies' themselves.

The virtually autonomous structure, granting a secular authority to the leaders of the confessional community, including fiscal and police powers, continued earlier practices, but was above all a mirror of the basic structure of the Muslim community itself. There again, as I have often had occasion to point out, this structure resulted not from a deliberate will of a divine Creator or a human founder, but from historical circumstances and conditions.

Yet it remains true that this politico-ideological structure ensured the survival and solidity of these communities down to the present day. It has also made the problems of integration into a more or less homogeneous nation-state more difficult. We see the dramatic consequences of this every day. The story is not ended.

It can be seen how necessary it is to get away from the contrasting ideological images that dominate opinion. On the one hand we have the picture of the Muslims and Islamophiles in which everything is for the best in the best of all possible worlds: Islam ensured untrammelled 'tolerance' of all differences, equality, goodness, freedom. On the other we see the image presented by the Islamophobes, who often border on racism: Islam pursued a perpetual and ferocious persecution of minorities.

We are not plunged into the realm of pure ideas which fight each other or agree, in the universe of ethereal essences of Evil-in-itself and Good-in-itself. Here, as elsewhere, we are dealing with the world of people with their passions, their interests and their visceral allegiance to the global structures to which they feel attached and towards which they feel a duty.

Notes

1. *A Dictionary of the Social Sciences*, ed. J. Gould and W. L. Kolb, London, Tavistock Publications, 1964, p. 433.

2. Every ideological formation with political power is driven to declare it. It is tempted to prohibit the teaching and dissemination of 'error' as soon as it can. 'What death more harmful for souls than the freedom granted to error?' (*quae peior mors animae, quam libertas erroris?*) said Saint Augustine (*epistola* 166) cited with approval and extended by Pope Gregory XVI in the encyclical *Mirari vos* of 15 August 1832 condemning Lamennais (Latin text of the passage in Denzinger, *Enchiridion symbolorum*, 31st ed., Friburgi Brisgoviae, Herder, 1957, no. 1614; French translation by G. Michon with other extracts in *Les documents pontificaux sur la démocratie et la société moderne*, Paris, Rieder, 1928, pp. 68—74).

3. The law of numbers reappears sometimes — although with some embarrassment — in states and ideological formations at the level of the definition of truth, when this is not (or not only) stated by a figure deemed infallible or does not emanate, as in Islam or Judaism, from many scholarly authorities giving qualified (and possibly contradictory) opinions on given points. Thus the Ecumenical Councils and communist Congresses pronounce an eternal truth by majority verdict. The latter, not being able to justify the authority of the majority by the inspiration of the Holy Spirit, have to fall back on a clever and complex selection of voters followed by an incoherent theorization on the charisma of so-called proletarian parties.

4. R. A. Schermerhorn, *These Our People...*, Boston, Heath, 1949, p. 5, quoted by *A Dictionary...*, p. 433.

5. I have attempted to situate these formations in an overall framework in my article 'Nations et idéologie' (*Encyclopaedia Universalis*, vol. XI, Paris, 1971, pp. 565—77).

6. The best synthesis is by Claude Cahen, in the article 'dhimma', in *Encyclopédie de l'Islam*, 2nd French ed., vol. II, Leyden (Brill) and Paris (Maisonneuve et Larose), 1965, pp. 234—8.

7. The 1918 constitution of the RSFSR (Russian Soviet Federative Socialist Republic) still recognized 'the freedom of religious and anti-religious propaganda' to all citizens (article 13). It was not mentioned in the 1924 constitution.

8. The indispensable concept of 'global society' was defined and developed by Georges Gurvitch. See particularly his books, *Déterminismes sociaux et liberté humaine*, Paris, PUF, 1955, pp. 195 et seq. and *La vocation actuelle de la sociologie*, vol. I, 4th ed., Paris, PUF, 1968, pp. 447 et seq.

9. Matthew, 12: 25; cf. Mark 3: 24—5; Luke, 11: 27.

10.   Lenin, 'The Dual Power', in *Pravda*, 9 April 1917, English translation in *Collected Works*, vol. 24, Moscow, Progress Publishers, 1964. See especially Lenin's pamphlet, 'Tasks of the Proletariat in Our Revolution', Petersburg, 1917, written in April, tr. in ibid. 'There is not the slightest doubt that such an "interlocking" *cannot* last long. Two powers *cannot exist* in a state. One of them is bound to pass away' (p. 61). The emphasis is Lenin's.

4
Empire and Minority
in China

FRANÇOIS THIERRY

Irrespective of its substance, the national question in China is a burning issue both for the Chinese and for those interested in the country because of its power to make or break the regime's reputation.

Chinese publications[1] show us an idyllic situation and endeavour to prove that the 'sister nationalities' have always united to build the Chinese state; others feel that modern China is behaving today as the Tang once did, as a colonial power; others again assure us that the policy of the People's Republic is radically new and that it has enabled it to settle the national question. Do the notions of national minority, nation-state, empire, ethnic group exist in Chinese history, and what policies have the Chinese leaders adopted to solve the problems that they embrace? If, as Balazs believes, history must be understood 'as the guide to bureaucratic practice',[2] it is a guide that is excellent for following the shifts of policy regarding the authority exercised over the non-Hans of China.

Traditional Chinese thought is based on two ideas, Order and Totality. Everything is one, and it is placed in a hierarchy, in a cosmic order, where its position is proportionate to its nature. To think of a national or ethnic minority, it is necessary, on the one hand, to think of a majority and a minority — that is two different beings — cohabiting in a common space, and on the other hand, to postulate the existence of a minimal common criterion that makes these different beings beings that are ontologically similar, that is to postulate that despite their difference they belong to humanity.

But for ancient Chinese philosophy, it is impossible to conceive of a common space for different beings and of the non-Hans as belonging to the human species.

Space is considered as square and is organized into overlapping squares whose nature is neither one nor undifferentiated. These are spaces ordered in a hierarchy distinguished by a difference of essence:

76

500 *li* constituted the Imperial domain ... Five hundred *li* beyond the Imperial domain constituted the domain of the nobles ... Five hundred *li* beyond the nobles' domain lay the peaceful domain ... Five hundred *li* beyond the peaceful domain was the domain of restraint. The first 300 were occupied by the I tribes, and the other 200 by criminals undergoing lesser banishment. Five hundred *li* beyond the domain of restraint lay the wild domain. Three hundred *li* were occupied by the Man tribes, and the other 200 *li* by criminals undergoing greater banishment.[3]

Real space, full space, only exists as socialized space, and the essence of socialization is the town: 'The square town of the Single Man, the capital, the centre of the world, opens on to it by four doors.'[4]

From these four doors the Virtue of the Prince shines out to the Four Easts, spreads over the world, civilizing the regions close by and gradually losing its effectiveness as it gets farther away from the Centre. It triumphs in the first four squares and then disappears in the wild zone, what the Chinese call the Four Seas, vast regions inhabited by the Four Species of Barbarians. This empty space can only bear incomplete, deformed or monstrous creatures, just as the full space can only bear men, Chinese, who, being alone equipped to live there, participate in its civilized nature. Thus the Barbarians could never dwell in the central squares; the only place granted them is the fringes of Civilization, as mediators with the wandering peoples. In ancient religion the serried ranks of aristocrats surrounded the Sacred Eminence in concentric circles according to their rank; representing the subject Barbarian lands, the tributary Barbarian chiefs belonging to the Domain of Restraint were arranged in an external square.[5] The appearance of the Barbarians in the Socialized Space is the sign of a disordered space, hence of a tottering princely Virtue and of a lack of harmony between the terrestrial order and the cosmic order. Conversely, the Chinese cannot live with impunity in the zones of emptiness, since they lose their nature there; that is why those who by their conduct have put themselves outside the norms of Civilization cannot remain in the central domains and must be sent to the periphery, to the Domain of Necessity. Banishment is one of the five basic punishments of Chinese justice, and, for centuries, criminals and convicts were sent to the fringes of the empire.

Since space is not homogeneous and undifferentiated, but arranged in a hierarchy according to its relations with the Centre, there cannot be any 'minority'; each person is in his or her place in the Order and there cannot be two essentially different beings in one and the same space. But the non-Hans are essentially different.

The basis of the difference between the Hans and the Barbarians was not originally of an ethnic nature, but rested on a relationship to Civilization, since for the Chinese there is Civilization and the Void. And the relevant criterion to establish this difference is sedentarization; the civilized one is the one who constructs towns and devotes himself to agriculture. What, in legend, formed the basis of the legitimate pretentions of the first king of the Zhou (1027 BC) was that his ancestor 'the old duke gave up the customs of the Rong and the Di [Barbarians]; for he built and raised up a rampart and a wall, houses and rooms; the town then became a separate place.'[6] The nature of Barbarians is to wander like animals in zones unsuited to sedentary culture such as steppes and mountains; animals are different from men precisely in that they have to wander in search of their subsistence, having only temporary lairs in which to rest their heads. Likewise with the Barbarians. This animal nature of the non-Hans was shown in their very name. The importance given in China to the harmony between the thing and its name is well known: every name must agree perfectly with the profound nature of what is named. Thus the graphic classification of the name of each type of Barbarian under a radical marking his animal nature is an ontological necessity. So one finds in the ideograms designating some Barbarians the root 'reptile' (the Mo, the Wei, the Lao, etc.), the root 'worm' (the Ruan, the Bie, the Dan, the Man, etc.) and above all the root 'dog' (the Di, the Yan, the Qiang, the Tong, etc.); some may be written equally with the root 'dog' or the root 'reptile' (the Wei, the Lao). This animal classification is sometimes replaced by classification under a radical 'grass' (the Mongols, the Liao, the Miao, the Lolo, etc.) which then stresses that they are linked to wild vegetation and not to agriculture, sedentarization. The term that is still used to describe the Barbarians, *yeman*, is composed of the character *man*, which we have seen above classified under the radical 'worm', and the character *ye*, which signifies 'rustic', 'wild', 'rude', 'non-urban', and by extension, 'who is not in power'.

Thus semantics gives us some exact indications: the Barbarians make no distinction between town and countryside, but wander about like animals. This view is particularly developed in ancient documents and especially in the *Shan Hai Jing*, a work of geography and ethnology dating from the period of the end of the Warring Kingdoms (second century BC).

The Jiao[7] are men who ornament themselves with tiger stripes and who wear rings around their calves on their legs; they live to the east of the territory of the Qiongqi; some say that they resemble men and they live rather to the north of the Kun Lun ... The Huanggu are men who have the head of a quadruped and the body of a man; some call them hedgehogs and say that they resemble dogs and that they are yellow.[8]

This denial of the humanity of others evolved over the centuries, but it underlay the relations that the Chinese formed with their neighbours. Thus we read about the aboriginal populations of south-western China, under the brush of an important official of the early Qing dynasty (seventeenth century), Wang Lüjie: 'These people are as simple as beasts and might even pass for monsters. But after all they are human beings . . .'[9]

It was on the basis of these two views, of the concentric and hierarchical nature of space and the sub-human character of the Other, that Chinese political practice rested initially in its relations with non-Hans.

In the Spring and Autumn period (771—481 BC), the concentric pattern worked well: in the Centre was the royal domain of the Zhou and beyond it stretched the domain of the old feudal houses, Chen, Lou, Song, etc., themselves bordered by rising great states, Qin, Jin, Chu, etc., that were half-Barbarian. But once all the cultivable lands had been occupied and unified (first century BC), the Chinese faced a contradiction in that they found themselves in direct contact with Barbarian peoples who were well adapted to their natural environment, whether it was the northern steppes or the southern forests. The Chinese empire then embarked on a policy of constructing around the strictly Chinese, strictly civilized lands a shield of tributary states, the aim of which was to avoid direct contact with Barbarism. These domains, integrated into the Chinese order, were not part of China; they were protected areas, a buffer between Barbarism and a Civilization whose Centre had to be protected.

The situation in the north and north-west was relatively simpler than in the south-west, even if it was much more worrying: the Barbarians of the steppes were spatially homogeneous when they came into contact with Civilization. The problem thus came down to organizing a protective belt around the Socialized Space by subjugating or buying off some tribes; under the Tang (618—907), for example, it was the Western Turks and then the Uighurs who protected the Centre against the Tibetans and the Tanguts. Chinese control of central Asia under the Han (206 BC—220 AD) or under the Tang was essentially a matter of foreign policy, the surveillance and control of the most dangerous nomads; there was no question of integrating these territories into the empire. Under the Tang in particular, the emperor Gao Zong (649—83) organized a system of five protectorates: Anxi over the Western Turks, Kun Ling to the south of lake Balkhash, Meng Chi over the Nu Shi Bi, Sogdiana and Tukhâristan in the far west.[10] These five protectorates subject to the empire were not governed by Chinese laws, and did not come under the civil administration of the Tang, whose western limit was at Dun Huang; there could be no question of the Barbarian states enjoying this essentially civilized form of social organization. These states were ruled by their rulers, according to their own laws, under the supervision of Chinese military garrisons, but there was not, at this time, any policy of colonization by settlement.[11] Naturally, in periods when the central government was weak, when a dynasty was declining or the territory was disintegrating, these allies turned against China, or made exorbitant demands in return for their neutrality.

In the south, the situation was much more complicated. Colonization occurred through the Hans seizing all the area suited to sedentary, irrigated farming, that is all the river plains and basins, the Yang zi, Xi jiang, Sichuan, the basin of the Red River, and the Great Lakes region, driving the aboriginal populations back into the mountains and the high valleys; thus a geographical distribution of populations came into being that was all the more confused and complicated because these south-western regions were the final eastern extension of the Himalayan chain, Yunnan, Sichuan, Guizhou, Huguang, Guangxi and even Fujian.

The Chinese empire thus found itself confronted with a heterogeneous space, which was inconceivable: in the Socialized Space there were pockets of Barbarism. What was required then was not so much self-protection, although these tribes continued to make raids against the Hans in the valleys until the dawn of the nineteenth century, but to ensure for the Socialized Space a homogeneity corresponding to that of Civilization. It was this homogeneity that was to be sought down to the present day by varying means and with varying degrees of success. The southern Barbarians (the generic terms were first Man and then Miao), who were especially scorned because they did not form state societies like the northern Barbarians, and were less organized and less dangerous, were the object of a policy that aimed at their assimilation, that is at their disappearance as Barbarians, or at their physical disappearance as a group.

This assimilation was implemented in two ways: administration through local chiefs or direct administration. These two policies were often used at the same time in several areas, or sometimes one after the other.[12]

Administration through local chiefs, a policy known by the name of *Yi yi zhi yi*, 'using the Barbarians to govern the Barbarians', began under the Hans, for example in the Red River delta, and lasted until the eighteenth century. Initially the newly conquered zones were administratively divided into autonomous districts and departments, the *jimi fou zhou*, 'departments and districts with the bridle on the neck', the leadership of which was entrusted to the former local authorities, or to Hans who had become integrated into the indigenous population, such as Zhao Tuo in Vietnam,[13] and who were integrated into the Chinese administrative system, and this was different from what happened in the north.

These local chiefs, the *Tu si*, 'administrators of the native peoples', governed their districts like petty kings. They were not paid by the public Treasury but lived off the country; their appointment was hereditary; and they were theoretically responsible only to the emperor, since they were rulers of small federated states. The *Tu si* were members of a special class of the general system of officials, but they came under the *Li bu*, the Ministry of the Civil Service. The existence of these hereditary and irremovable officials was of course shocking to Chinese officials as a whole, and it was one of the points of attack by the supporters of direct administration. The policy of the *Tu si*, which was really rather liberal, made it possible to maintain at low cost a relative calm on the southern and south-western frontiers, but it aimed above all at the assimilation of the Barbarians through the assimilation of the elites. The *Tu si* and their entourages adopted Chinese customs, settled in *yamen*, and became sedentarized; schools were opened by the Hans for the children of the local aristocracy, with the Imperial Treasury taking over responsibility for paying the costs of schooling. To oblige these children to attend these schools, it was laid down that the post of *Tu si* could only be inherited by someone, male or female, educated in the Chinese school; the brightest children of the aristocracy were called to pursue their studies in the provincial capitals, or even in the Capital itself. On the other hand, the *Tu si* were obliged to make available aboriginal troops to the provincial governor in the event of disturbances, and this was particularly important in periods when dynasties were declining.[14]

In fact, to a great extent, the *Tu si* remained autonomous and took advantage of these periods of weakness of Chinese authority to take back from the Hans lands seized by force or to redeem debts in earlier years. Some local chiefs, like the Yi of the An clan, remained *de facto* independent from the third century to the beginning of the Qin in the seventeenth in the west of Guizhou.[15] Around the Bai tribes, the state of Nan Zhao was organized in the eighth century; it survived in Yunnan, sometimes as tributary, sometimes as enemy of China, until the arrival of the Mongols in 1254.[16]

This policy of indirect rule, either through the intermediary of a protectorate or with the system of *Tu si*, only functioned when the Chinese central government was strong, or, to speak like the Chinese, when the princely Virtue shone forth. If for some reason or other the Centre was weakened, the edifice collapsed; this is what happened at the end of the Qin dynasty (221-206 BC), the Han and the Tang, but after this last dynasty, the Chinese central government was never able to reorganize its concentric system as it wanted. Worse still, whole areas of the Socialized Space were occupied by the Barbarians for centuries until the time when the whole of China was subjected to the Mongols in the thirteenth century. For the Chinese, this tragedy led to a fundamental rethinking of ideas about political rule.

During periods when the empire was weak, the Barbarians moved to occupy large areas of China, mainly in the north and north-west. For the Hans, this irruption of the Barbarians into the Socialized Space was the sign that the harmony was upset, but for the Mongols these concepts meant nothing.

The populations of the north-west and north, generally nomads or semi-nomads, were organized into hierarchical societies on the basis of military, clan and feudal criteria: the lands belonged to the clan aristocracy which organized the movement of flocks and the associated economic activities, and led the tribes or the confederation of tribes, through a direct democracy in the military body, with a structure of vassalage which varied from group to group, Mongols, Turks, Tanguts, Kitans, Jurchen, etc. For these peoples, the conquered territory belonged to the tribe which disposed of it freely according to its own internal rules, the nomad conqueror lording it over the defeated sedentary people.

The forms of political domination varied because some Barbarians adopted Chinese practices with their customs, particularly in the earliest periods, as under the Wei dynasty, founded in AD 386 by the Taba Tatar tribes. But the widely accepted idea that each wave of Barbarians was assimilated by the defeated Hans must be treated carefully since it is clear that 'conquest dynasties'[17] organized to resist Chinese pressures, usually by instituting ethnic discrimination.

In the tenth century, Kitan tribes, proto-Mongols, settled in the north of the Huang He valley. At about the same time, the Tanguts, nomads of Tibetan origin, occupied the north-west. In the twelfth century, the Jurchen, proto-Manchu nomads, occupied the whole of the north of China and finally, in the thirteenth century, the Mongols overran the whole of the country. This created a new situation, with an ethnic minority dominating the enormous mass of Chinese peasants. This minority had then to organize its domination in such a way that its own ethnic, religious, social, and other characteristics should always be distinguished from those of the defeated populations.

The Liao state founded by the Kitans, for example, drew up a code of laws in 921 that were different according to whether they applied to the nomads, the Kitans and their allies, or the Hans;[18] similarly, the

Liao territories were administered according to different laws in the northern home area of the Kitans and in the Chinese southern area. The Jurchen, who founded the Jin dynasty, did the same when they first established themselves in northern China. However, it was the Mongols who pushed this practice of racial discrimination to its logical conclusion, no doubt because they were organized in a more military and more centralized way than their predecessors.

They applied Mongol martial law to the conquered territories, which meant that the whole administration was handed over to the army and the military leaders who were also tribal chiefs. For a time, at the beginning of the conquest under Genghis Khan, there was even a suggestion of reducing the whole of north China to the state of steppes, destroying the towns so that the Mongol tribes could nomadize there. Finally attracted by the potential wealth of agriculture, the Mongol leaders decided to administer the country by the methods of the Liao and the Jin, stressing the separation between nomads and Hans. The Mongol codes, reworked several times, divided society into four groups arranged in a hierarchy according to their ethnic background: at the top were the Mongols, then the 'foreigners', *se mu*, that is the other allied nomads, and the Arab, Persian, Sogdianan, European and other foreigners, then the *han ren*, including the Koreans, the Kitans, the Jurchen and their formers subjects in north China, and finally, at the bottom of the scale, the *nan ren*, the Chinese, former subjects of the Southern Song.[19] This code was based on inequality between the races: there were special laws for the Mongols and special tribunals,[20] some administrative positions were barred to Hans, even in junior positions, non-Chinese were given favoured treatment in examinations,[21] and the use of the Mongol script in the administration was imposed while the Chinese were banned from studying it.[22] The civil administration was paralleled by a military administration which in order to ensure its power over the Chinese population and control it better, divided it into groups of twenty households headed by a Mongol who enjoyed every privilege over those he administered, including that of having sexual relations with any young woman he wanted.[23]

This occupation, even when softened at the end of the dynasty (1277—1367), was based on notions of social organization, political sovereignty and Space that were foreign to the Chinese. The Mongols governed the country militarily as their own domain, conceiving of it as an empire within whose borders no autonomous areas could be tolerated. Whereas the Chinese conceived political domination in terms of the Power of the Centre radiating outwards in successive decreasing zones, which ruled out the notion of frontiers in the modern sense of the word, the Mongols conceived their domains as a military empire with frontiers and internal homogeneity. This is why, for example, the Mongols pursued a much more aggressive policy towards the aboriginal populations of the south-west, destroying the federated state of Nan Zhao in 1254 and setting up a military administration, the 'Office for the Pacification of the Eight Barbarian Tribes of Shun Yuan',[24] established in the heart of the autonomous zones. This office produced only limited results because of the growing difficulties of the Mongol Yuan dynasty in other parts of the empire, but the idea of a more military approach to the problem was born.

For a century, the Centre, the Interior, *nei*, was occupied by the Barbarians who ensured their rule over the Chinese through racial discrimination; as a reaction, Han 'nationalism' appeared.

Previously the difference between Civilization and Barbarism had been independent of ethnic membership; a Barbarian who became sedentarized benefited from the illumination of Civilization and became a Chinese, that is a man. From the end of the Yuan, however, there emerged the notion of ethnic membership, of racial solidarity *vis-à-vis* the foreign occupiers and the idea of an unbreakable relationship between the Han race and Chinese civilization which underpinned the Hans' feeling of superiority over other races. Similarly, the idea of an empire enclosed within frontiers began to make headway at the expense of the old idea of an Order of hierarchical spaces arranged around the civilized Centre. So it was no accident that the Ming dynasty (1367–1644) which succeeded the Mongols rebuilt the Great Wall in the north to make it a proper frontier between the empire and the nomads, and in the south built a wall over two hundred kilometres long to mark off what was and what was not China. Obsessed by the danger of the nomads to the north, the Ming scarcely sought to find solutions to the problem of the aboriginal areas which survived in the south. At the beginning of the dynasty, the government set up military colonies, the *tun dian*, in order to contain the most turbulent tribes and promote Han colonization; it maintained the system of *Tu si* while promoting as much as possible the attachment of the autonomous districts to direct administration[25] through intensive colonization, a policy which in the sixteenth and seventeenth centuries provoked an interminable and cruel simmering war between the Hans and the mountain peoples.

Chinese thought in the Ming period was marked by a formalist reaction which led to solutions to contemporary problems being sought by looking to the past and by the appearance of Chinese 'nationalism'. This ideological enclosure in the past was now accompanied by a diplomatic enclosure just when a massive redrawing of the map was beginning around the empire. The Spanish were in the Philippines, the Portuguese in Macao, the Dutch in Indonesia and Formosa, the Japanese were making major forays in the direction of Korea and the Russians were advancing into Siberia and towards northern Manchuria. The pieces were falling into place that would finally render the traditional conception of Space null and void; the fall of the Ming under the attacks of the Manchu tribes, which founded a new dynasty, the Qing, in 1644, and the consolidation of this conquest dynasty marked the beginning of the 'obscure turn' in policy towards the non-Hans in China.

Like the Mongols, the Manchus were former nomads who had become sedentarized on the north-eastern frontiers of China. They were organized in a military empire on the basis of tribal division and took forty years to conquer the whole of Ming China, the Eighteen Provinces; they established a military government there based on the famous Banners, whose aim was to ensure for the Manchu clans domination over the mass of Chinese. Once again, it was an ethnic minority that seized supreme power.[26]

The Manchus' conception of political authority, bearing the imprint of 'tribal despotism' or 'military feudalism' comparable to that of the Mongols, evolved rapidly through the assimilation of some Chinese ideas (central administration, officials subject to dismissal) and through contact with Westerners, mainly Jesuits, who became integrated into the body of scholars and introduced into it the notions of state and frontier, but also under the pressure of outside events. The empty Space around China was growing smaller and smaller, especially in the north where the Russians had reached the Sea of Okhotsk in 1645 and the Amur river in Manchuria in 1653. The new dynasty found itself obliged to discuss the respective borders of the two empires in terms of Western political science, leading to the Treaty of Nerchinsk in 1689.

This was an important date marking the end of the traditional conception of the Chinese Space. After Nerchinsk, the elites were forced to admit the necessity of building a unitary state, all parts of which would depend equally on the centre of power, the emperor. It was no longer a question of building a shield of tributary states, more or less federated, but of building a whole, the empire of China, for whose protection the colonization, integration and assimilation of the peripheral zones were necessary.

To ward off the Western Mongols, who, under the leadership of the Dzungarians were advancing eastward, the Manchus embarked on the conquest of Tarim and Turkestan. To oversee this policy, a regular Colonial Office was created, the *Li Fan Yuan* (Secretariat for the

Government of the Marches) which was raised to the same rank as ministries in 1661.[27] The first act was the war waged by the Kang Xi emperor (1662–1723) and then the Qian Lung emperor (1736–1796) against the Dzungarian Oïraths, which ended in 1760 with the conquest of Illi and the Tarim basin and the general massacre of the Dzungarians.[28]

The conquered areas were immediately organized into a special system of government: Mongolia was divided into three zones, Inner, Outer and Illi, access to which was forbidden to Hans; they were governed by an imperial resident, the *amban*; the traditional power of the Mongol khans, even allied ones (Eastern Mongols, Khalkhas), was broken by the destruction of Mongol feudalism, in favour of a new hierarchy of direct vassalage to the Manchu emperor. Against the khans, the Qing mobilized and supported the Lamaist monasteries of the Yellow Bonnet Sect; Mongol customary law was replaced by the Qing code, the cultural heritage was suppressed, Mongol books were burned, etc. Every sign of rebellion was bloodily put down in the name of the higher interest of the empire.[29]

Turkestan, from which it was possible to control the Mongols from the west and the south, became the New Frontier. Called *Xin Jiang*, Turkestan was a zone of colonization reserved initially for the Manchus alone. Soon, Manchus from the Amur, Chahar and Jehol were being sent there in large numbers to garrison the military colonies and even Hans, including many convicts, were authorized to colonize Dzungaria, now emptied of its inhabitants. The Manchus then allowed them to settle anywhere in Turkestan. The Muslim, Uighur, Kazakh or Tadjik peoples of these regions watched powerlessly as colonization was organized. The whole of Xin Jiang was under military administration by the Manchus without a single Chinese official, as it was intended to keep this territory under the direct authority of the Manchu government.

At the same time, the regions of origin of the dynasty were divided into three provinces, Jilin, Heilung Jiang and Liaoning, governed by traditional Manchu law and coming directly under the emperor as the head of the federated Manchu clans. Access to these regions was forbidden to Hans.[30] The policy of the Qing towards the aboriginal peoples of the south-west rested on the idea of a unitary empire and thus aimed at the disappearance of the autonomous zones, in accordance with European views:

The existence of a free and independent people, like these mountaineers, in the bosom of an empire so powerful as China, may appear extraordinary to the politicians of Europe. Perhaps they may say, How is it possible, that emperors, whose wisdom and zeal for the good of the public have been so much extolled, should have suffered this nation of free-booters to exist for so long?[31]

We can see how the idea of the nation-state, present in the Jesuit advisers of the first Qing emperors, was injected into Chinese political thought. To this idea was added the introduction of an economistic way of thinking: it was no longer a matter of ensuring a theoretical domination over the autonomous zones in order to guarantee peace on the frontiers, it was a matter of exercising a real authority over territories with abundant resources which were beginning to run short in the lands already colonized:

> For hundreds of years the peoples have had good lands, but they do not know how to develop them; they have reserves of timber but do not know how to use them; they have precious mineral resources but do not know how to exploit them.[32]

wrote the mandarin Wang Lüjie, who proposed replacing the *Tu si* by officials subject to dismissal. The imperial government and the administration endeavoured to conquer and subjugate the aboriginals and bring them under the administrative common law: this policy was called *Gai tu gui liu*, replacing local chiefs with officials subject to dismissal. The colonial war lasted from the late seventeenth to the early nineteenth century with a pitiless ferocity and tenacity on the part of the Manchus, who initially organized the occupied lands:

> When the lands have just been confiscated, it is not suitable to give them straight to civilians; but when the soldiers have been there for some time, and thus confirmed the taking of possession, it is possible to hand them over to civilians.[33]

The civilians mentioned were Han settlers who were settled in the districts thus brought under civil administration. Then the policy of assimilation was applied to the local populations by dismantling the traditional society.

The Miaos, who by custom always bore arms, were disarmed and any Miao found carrying arms (arbalest, bow, as well as gun) was executed as a rebel; customary justice was replaced by the Qing code to which was added a special repressive law; they were deported, or sedentarized by force. A network of military strongpoints was organized to penetrate further into the mountains and pave the way for Han colonization. This policy of colonization of areas where non-Hans lived, except for Tibet whose climate and altitude the Chinese never liked, and integration was a constant feature of the Manchu dynasty which considered the empire as the unitary domain of the emperor of China.

The traditional categories began to fade away as China was integrated into the world market. Paradoxically, it was a non-Chinese, Manchu dynasty that gave birth to the idea of a Chinese state in the modern sense of the word and gradually took up the historical heritage of Chinese dynasties. The Chinese state in practice made so many concessions to the Western states in the very areas that are traditionally the responsibility of the state (customs, railways, territorial sovereignty, etc.) that, in order to gain the maximum out of these concessions, the Westerners carrying out these functions pushed the Chinese government to organize its country and its state on the Western model.

The repression of the Muslim revolt in Turkestan (1862—1878) was done in the name of the integrity of the territory of the nation. Any attack on part of the empire was seen as an attack on the whole. 'If Xinjiang is not secure, there will be unrest in Mongolia; then, it is not only Shenxi, Gansu and Shanxi which will be disturbed, it is also the sleep of the population of the nation's capital,' wrote the Imperial Commissioner Zo Zongtang in 1877.[34] After the crushing of the revolt and the period of repression (military government, deportation, massacres, etc.),[35] Xinjiang became a Chinese province subject to the common law and a land of colonization.

The power of the Westerners in the state apparatus, the administration and the economy, made the Manchu leaders, as well as the Reformers, well aware of the relevance of the European concept of the modern centralized, unitary state. Paradoxically, the imperialist nations played (according to their goals) on both the centralization and the break-up of the empire: Western exploitation of the customs, ports and railways required a policy of unification, whereas the theory of spheres of influence strengthened separatism. The Russians paid court to the Uighurs in Xinjiang, the British to the Tibetans, the French to the people of Yunnan, and the Japanese, after defeating the Russians, supported the virtually autonomous power of the governor of Manchuria.

The voracity of the Europeans and the inability of the Qing to resist them led to the 'revolution' of 1911. The fall of the empire opened a period of disintegration of China which ended only in 1949 when the communist state of Yanan defeated the Republic of China of the Guomin Dang and conquered the whole of the territory. For those who initiated the 1911 'revolution', for the intellectuals, particularly for all those who were behind the explosion of the May 4th Movement[36] — Sun Yat Sen, Chen Duxiu, Huang Xing, Hu Shi and Cai Yuanpei — the national question was seen in terms of oppressed China versus imperialist nations. The problem of the oppressed nations of the empire was completely passed over; it was a time for anti-imperialism, the reappropriation of Chinese identity stifled by the appetites of Europeans, who had been helped by the foreign power of the Manchu court.

Dr Sun Yat Sen's *San Minzhu Yi*,[37] the theoretical basis of the Guomin Dang, never mentions the problem of national minorities. Dr Sun speaks of the 'Chinese people' and the 'Chinese peasant' as sharing in a transnational citizenship. The Three Principles of the People are Nationalism, the Power of the People and the Welfare of the People: it is by introducing egalitarian democracy that all the problems will be solved. Science and democracy are the keywords of republican discourse, and nowhere in the 1924 lectures, which together make up the *San Minzhu Yi*, is there any mention of the right of peoples to self-determination: all the inhabitants of China are Chinese citizens, equal in rights and duties like French citizens in France. The republican government once in power found itself faced with a theoretical contradiction: how to make a nation-state when there are several nations in the state? The response was simple: do away with the nations!

> With the present government which has the Triple Demism as its banner, if we do not succeed in introducing our culture among these peoples and getting them to fuse with us, we may despair forever of seeing the union of the races of our country.[38]

It is true that from 1919–20 onwards, those claiming to rule China faced other issues, the first being the *de facto* disappearance of the country through its break-up into rival principalities, independent provinces and puppet states. In fact, taking advantage of the collapse of central authority and the multiplication of self-proclaimed 'Chinese governments', the peripheral regions took their freedom, sometimes with the more or less disinterested assistance of great neighbours. Britain protected the independence of Tibet; in Manchuria the Japanese supported the secession led by Zhang Zolin, on whose death they organized the state of Manchukuo, and they also fuelled those in Mongolia advocating independence; the Russians promoted the accession to independence of Outer Mongolia and advised the governor of Xinjiang, where they moved in and launched a minorities policy on the Soviet model, which advocated teaching in the local language and the real representation of the local peoples in provincial bodies.

If the Guomin Dang, then its government, had scarcely thought about the national question and had failed to grasp its importance, the same was not true of the Chinese Communist Party, which had the benefit of the theoretical achievements of the Second and Third Internationals.

Created in 1921, the Chinese Communist Party was peculiar in that it did not emerge from a social-democractic or nationalist party, but from the coming together of a number of figures whose essential motivation was the renovation, modernization and emancipation of China, all goals which in themselves had no 'class content'. The creation of the Chinese Communist Party was the direct result of Chinese sympathy for Soviet Russia and its anti-imperialist attitude towards China; in 1920, in Peking, the Yurin mission solemnly renounced the Unequal Treaties and the indemnity arising from the Boxer rebellion. This non-proletarian character of the initial aims of the Chinese communists helps to explain the ease with which they entered into the Guomin Dang on the orders of the Communist International in 1924. The birth of a 'true' Marxist-Leninist party dates from the time when, rejected by its previous allies at the time of the crushing of the unions and workers in Shanghai in 1927, the leadership of the CCP was obliged to join Mao Zedong and Chu De's Red Base in Jiangxi province and apply the 'class versus class' tactic.[39] In the revolutionary struggle, the problem of national minorities then played a not insignificant role.

In order to establish its tactics in this area, the CCP had to take account both of the state of the debate on this question in the communist movement and of the orientation of Soviet foreign policy, which used the Comintern as a parallel diplomatic structure.

Without going back over the debate that marked the London congress of the Second International (1896),[40] we can say briefly that the national question shifted from being a matter of principle with Kautsky to being a matter of tactics with Lenin and Trotsky: the former proclaimed the right of peoples to self-determination, whereas the latter, with Rosa Luxemburg,[41] considered that this right could and should not be an unbreakable principle, but was subordinate to tactical considerations. Self-determination, said Lenin and Trotsky, must be used as a transitional, agitational slogan and care must be taken to avoid the ravages that the national idea might produce by introducing the idea of separation among the workers of multinational states such as Russia and Austria.[42] With the Russian revolution, the tactical character of the right of peoples to self-determination appeared in practice; the Caucasian affair (in 1921, the Red Army invaded Georgia) gave Leon Trotsky the opportunity to set things out clearly:

We support with all our strength the principle of the right of peoples to self-determination where it is directed against feudal, capitalist or imperialist states. But where the fiction of national autonomy is transformed in the hands of the bourgeoisie into a weapon directed against the revolution of the proletariat, we have no reason to treat it any differently than the other principles of democracy transformed into their opposite by Capital.[43]

The Chinese Communist Party, a section of the Comintern, made the tactical conception of the national question its own. Driven out by the Guomin Dang armies, the CCP built up in the province of Jiangxi a state apparatus and drew up a constitution for the Republic of Chinese Soviets, which was promulgated at the first Congress of Chinese Soviets at Ruichin on 7 November 1931. It stated:

The Soviet government of China recognizes the right of self-determination of the national minorities in China, their right to complete separation from China and to the formation of an independent state for each national minority. All, Mongolians, Tibetans, Miao, Yao, Koreans, and others living on the territory of China shall enjoy the full right to self-determination, i.e. they may either join the Union of Chinese Soviets or secede from it and form their own state as they may prefer.[44]

This stand (after reading Trotsky, one may doubt the degree to which it was a principled stand) was an excellent agitational slogan, and during the Long March the Red Armies received assistance from the minority peoples on the borders of Tibet which enabled them to reach Yanan. But, being tactical, it was subject to the strategic plan of the Centre, in this case the interests of the Russian Soviet state; what was revolutionary and politically right was what was good for Russia. So when after 1933 Stalin began a *rapprochement* with the democracies against Germany, the 'class versus class' tactic was abandoned in favour of the formation of popular fronts.[45] The CCP then had to join with the Guomin Dang and the state apparatus of the Republic of China in a United Front Against Japan (1937) to liberate the country and create a 'United Chinese Democratic Republic'.[46] The question of minorities receded before the need to maintain the integrity of the bourgeois nation-state.[47] At the same time, the rehabilitation by Stalin in 1934–5 of the 'Russian Fatherland' and the exaltation of its leading role in the Soviet Union were factors that in the CCP strengthened Great-Han chauvinism in a Jacobin conception of the 'empire'. Even before the victory of 1949 (and even more after) the communists were posing as the heirs to the historic rights of China over the whole of the former territories of the Manchu empire. It can be said that the People's Republic of China's conception of the national question emerged directly from this period of the Communist International; it was not a matter of constructing, as in Russia in 1918, a Union of Soviets, a Union of Chinese Soviet Republics, but of organizing a united communist state under the leadership of the Han nation:

> In order to strengthen the unity of the fatherland and the unity of the nationalities, in order to build the country as one great family, where there will be full equality and regional autonomy for the nationalities, the minority peoples will be aided so as to undertake social reforms and to develop their economy, their policy and their culture; thus, those who are backward will be able to catch up with those who are advanced in the transition to socialism.[48]

Here we find one of the recurrent themes of totalitarian ideology: since the people are one, its expression is one and its representation must be one. The unity of society stands against the heterogeneous, what cannot be recognized, and its norm is the Han people, united as the vanguard in the socialist transformation of society, a position which 'scientifically' underpins the hegemonic pretentions of the Hans in the process that leads to the homogenization of society in China. The minorities 'must first of all learn and absorb the science and advanced culture of the principal nationality of our fatherland, and ensure for itself the help of the Han people.'[49] Han assistance, however, was more like colonial exploitation than anything else:

> I said that China could not do without its minority nationalities. There are scores of nationalities in China. The regions inhabited by the minority nationalities are more extensive than those inhabited by the Han nationality and abound in material wealth of all kinds. Our national economy cannot do without the economy of the minority nationalities.[50]

While noting the similarity of the tone of this thought of Mao Zedong to that of the Manchu mandarin quoted above, we can see the importance of Marxist economic arguments in strengthening the tendencies towards unification. Any manifestation by a nationality, or by some of its members, of its difference is an attack against the unity of China in transition to socialism, against socialism and thus against the direction of history. 'Any secessionist attempt by a nationality would be contrary to the tendency of extended historical development and to its basic needs.'[51] The

Chinese leaders will only be satisfied when the nationalities as such have disappeared.

The whole of Chinese policy from 1949 right down to the present day has been aimed at unification, that is, assimilation. The methods have changed from terrorist to liberal according to the 'radical' or 'pragmatic' periods that mark the history of the PRC — 'pragmatic' from 1949 to 1957 and since 1978, and 'radical' between 1958 and 1976 — but the goal is still assimilation.

The People's Republic set up Autonomous Regions and Districts — in Mongolia, as early as 1947 — and administrative and territorial structures that were supposed to ensure for each minority the exercise of its national rights. At first, to weld the country together again, the traditional elites were used, with the promise that social reforms would be minimal.[52] In fact, real power passed into the hands of the Hans through the use of a variety of instruments: party and military hierarchies, the implementation of a policy of sinification, the strengthening of garrisons, the peopling by Hans of minority zones, the appointment of Hans to all decision-making posts in administration, education, health, etc., and the preparation of a plan based on purely nationalist goals. The Communist Party soon came to be seen as the instrument of Han nationalism. All these grievances exploded at the time of the Hundred Flowers,[53] but the Chinese bureaucracy swung to the left: the policy of assimilation was stepped up and made more systematic. Just as the Great Proletarian Cultural Revolution accelerated the socialist revolution, the unification of the working people of the whole country had to make a leap forward, all the more so as the regions inhabited by national minorities were along the frontier where China's new enemy, 'Soviet social-imperialism', was posing a threat to national unity. There then developed a whole literature derived from the ideology of national security to justify the maintenance of the minority nationalities in the People's Republic and the taking over by the Hans of the running of the autonomous regions, since the Hans had absolutely no confidence in the Uighurs' or Tibetans' ability to defend the nation — a nation that, in the last analysis, was not theirs. Since 1978, it would seem that the leadership of the Communist Party has reverted to the softly softly method.

In the framework of this essay we do not intend to assess the effects of this policy minority by minority,[54] but we will show, using the Mongolian case, how the Chinese leaders understand the resolution of the national question.

In 1947, the communists set up the Autonomous Region of Mongolia under the leadership of Ulanfu, a local communist leader. At this time there were three Chinese for every Mongolian in the territory. In the liberal phase (1949—57), the Communist Party systematically favoured Hans in jobs, divided the autonomous region into autonomous sub-departments based on minorities in the minority and so detaching territories from the original region, organized Han colonization by grants of equipment and foodstuffs and facilities for settlement in the grasslands of the pastoral populations, etc. By 1957, therefore, the proportion had risen to eight Chinese for every Mongolian. At the time of the Hundred Flowers, several leaders protested, and Ulanfu was purged for 'local nationalism'. The policy of assimilation was stepped up to such a point that by 1971 there were, in the Autonomous Region of Mongolia, fifteen Chinese for every Mongolian.[55] Thus today the population of the Autonomous Region of 'Mongolia' is only six per cent Mongolian! It may be wondered why there is any need to maintain this territorial division. The past of Mongolia is the present of Xinjiang and no doubt the future of Tibet.

Finally, we should stress one point in the discourse of the Chinese communists: the amalgamation of nation and minority. By embracing in the same term, *minzu*, nation, nationality, national groups as different as the Heche minority (800 souls) and the Uighur nation (5.4 million), Chinese theoreticians gloss over the debate between national rights and minority rights. The same solution cannot be given to the problem of the existence of nations such as the Tibetans or the Uighurs, who have a history, a language, a territory of their own and above all a national consciousness, and the problem posed by ethnic groups made up of a few thousand people, such as the Baoan, the Ewenke, the Jingpo, etc. By placing the debate on the level of nationalities in general, the Chinese communists are treating what are several questions as one and suggesting that it requires a single solution. On the pretext of equal treatment of all minorities, the Han majority is imposing on the most stubborn nations the same treatment as the most open ones.

However, the present 'pragmatic' phase is making possible a 'liberation of thinking', a liberation which is certainly very timid, but which nevertheless exists. Thus, on the question we are concerned with, problematics are appearing that link up with research conducted in Western countries, such as that on the 'punished peoples' which Fei Xiaodong applies to the Tujias of Hunan, a minority that was denied any rights after liberation because it had been used by the central government to keep down other minorities.[56]

Three conceptions of empire, and hence of minority, have guided the practice of the states that have followed one another in China: a traditional conception, based on a hierarchy of spaces, a military conception, deriving from the conquest dynasties, which were of nomadic origin, and a Jacobin conception, ending in its 'socialist' avatar.

But beyond superficial similarities in practice, what must be stressed is how fundamentally divergent the traditional conception and the *Mao-socialist* conception are. Traditional Chinese philosophy thought of the Totality as the interaction of complementary opposites:

> The whole world recognizes the beautiful as the beautiful, yet this is only the ugly; the whole world recognizes the good as the good, yet this is only the bad.
> Thus something and nothing produce each other.
> The difficult and the easy complement each other.
> The long and the short offset each other.
> The high and the low incline towards each other.
> Note and sound harmonize with each other.
> Before and after follow each other.[57]

Paraphrasing Lao Zi, one could say that the whole world recognized Civilization as Civilization, yet this is only Barbarism. To try to eliminate Barbarism in the space assigned to it means provoking a breach of the natural harmony. Such was the position defended by the Scholars who in 81 BC opposed the military expeditions of the Han emperors against the Huns.

> The Huns live in the midst of the desert, on an inhospitable land, abandoned by the sky and by men. They have no real homes and do not practice separation of the sexes. The horizons of the vast steppes are the streets of their towns and hair tents are their houses. They dress themselves in skins and furs, eat only meat, and know no other beverage than the blood of animals. Their way of life which only brings them together so as to disperse them again, makes them like the does and the deer in our country. But warmongering ministers, by requiring them to bend to our way of life, have lit the flames of war throughout the empire.[58]

Conversely, in the civilized space, Barbarism had to be subjugated not by force but by the illumination of virtue, by inaction, *wu wei*:

> At the time of the Chun emperor, the princes of Miao refused to submit. His son-in-law Yu the Great wanted to put them down by force. But Chun persuaded him to abandon this proposal: It is because my virtue is not yet exemplary, he said. He went into retreat and devoted himself to perfecting his government. Then the people of the Miaos made its submission. A good monarch does not use force against a rebellious people.[59]

Seeking to act against the course of things is contrary to the natural operation of the mutations that brings about all change as a result of transformations, *bian hua*. Marxism on the other hand claims to be a philosophy of action, of the conscious action of the proletariat through a revolutionary party, for the building of a radically new world, a *project* that demands the total victory of one over the other(s). This unique moment, this radical break, is revolution, after which 'nothing will ever be the same again.' The mission of the proletariat necessitates its unity, its cohesion: being One, its expression is One and its representation One:

> We must use Mao tse-tung's thought to unify the thinking of the whole Party and the thinking of the people of the whole country ... We must turn the whole country into a great school of Mao tse-tung's thought. We must build our great motherland into a still more powerful and prosperous country. This is the demand of the Chinese people as well as the hope placed in us by the people of all countries. Long live the *people* of all the nationalities of China! Long live the great unity of the people of the world![60]

This totalitarian unification presupposes the disappearance of every heterogeneous element; hence the disappearance of the *peoples* of the different nations of China.

Notes

1. Among the most recent: Fei Hsiao Tung, *Toward a People's Anthropology*, Peking, New World Press, 1981, and also *Zhongguo minzu guanxi shi* (History of the relations between the nationalities of China), Lanzhou, Institute of Nationalities of Gansu, 1983.
2. Etienne Balazs, *La bureaucratie céleste*, Paris, Gallimard NRF, 1968, p. 47.
3. Qian Sima, *Mémoires historiques*, tr. Chavannes, Paris, E. Leroux, 1905, vol. 1, p. 146 (this translation by Herbert J. Allen, 'ssuma Ch'ien's Historical Records, Chapter II: The Hsia Dynasty', in *Journal of the Royal Asiatic Society*, 1895).
4. Marcel Granet, *Danses et légendes de la Chine ancienne*, Paris, F. Alcan, 1926, p. 249.
5. Ibid., pp. 231 et seq.
6. Qian Sima, *Mémoires historiques*, vol. 1, ch. IV, p. 215.
7. *Jiao* is also the name of a poisonous insect, as *huanggu*, mentioned below, means 'yellow dog'.
8. Rémi Mathieu, *Etude sur la Mythologie et l'Ethnologie de la Chine ancienne*, annotated translation of the *Shan Hai Jing*, Paris, Mémoires de l'IHEC, 1983, chap. XII, p. 489.
9. Claudine Lombard-Salmon, *Un exemple d'acculturation chinoise. La province du Guizhou au XVIIIe siècle*, 3rd cycle thesis, Paris VII, 1968, p. 202.
10. *The Cambridge History of China*, vol. III, *Sui and T'ang China*, Cambridge, Cambridge University Press, 1981, p. 281.

11. Several centuries later the Tai Zu emperor of the Ming (1368–99) synthesized this conception by writing: 'The Barbarians are left outside, but they are subject to the Middle Kingdom', in *Huang Ming wen heng*, quoted by Albert Chan, *The Glory and Fall of the Ming Dynasty*, Oklahoma University Press, 1982, p. 378.

12. We will deal with direct rule as the policy was modified under the Qing (1644–1911), since it was this dynasty that applied this policy most strictly. It can be said that, broadly, indirect rule was dominant until the seventeenth century.

13. Le Thanh Khoi, *Histoire du Vietnam, dès origines à 1858*, Paris, Sudestasie, 1981, pp. 81-2.

14. James B. Parsons, *Peasant Rebellions of the Late Ming Dynasty*, P. Wheatley, Association for Asian Studies, no. XXVI, 1970, pp. 51 and 239.

15. Lombard-Salmon, *Un exemple d'acculturation chinoise*, pp. 126 et seq.

16. Michael Blackmore, 'The rise of Nan Chao in Yunnan', in *Journal of South East Asian History*, 1, 2 (1960), pp. 47-61.

17. Karl Wittfogel, *Oriental Despotism*, New Haven, Yale University Press, 1957.

18. Karl Wittfogel and Chiaseng Feng, *History of Chinese Society—Liao*, Philadelphia, American Philosophic Society, 1949, p. 576.

19. Ratchnevsky, *Un code des Yuan*, Paris, E. Leroux, 1937, p. 30.

20. Ibid., p. 274.

21. Ibid., p. xxvii, Introduction.

22. Charles O. Hucker, *The Ming Dynasty: its Origins and Evolving Institutions*, Michigan University Press, 1978, p. 3.

23. Ibid., p. 4.

24. Lombard-Salmon, *Un exemple d'acculturation chinoise*, p. 37.

25. Charles O. Hucker, *Chinese Government in Ming Times*, New York, Columbia University Press, 1969, p. 4.

26. It is estimated that 186,000 troops took part in the invasion of China in 1644, of whom 96,000 were Eight Bannermen Manchus. Cf. Djang Chu Wen, *The Moslem Rebellion in North-West China, 1862–1878*, Taipeh, Rainbow Bridge Book, 1966, p. 10.

27. Lawrence D. Kessler, *K'ang Hsi and the Consolidation of Ching Rule, 1661–1684*, Chicago, Chicago University Press, 1976, p. 30.

28. Djang Chu Wen, *The Moslem Rebellion*, Ch. 1. Eighty per-cent of the Dzungarians disappeared at this time, the rest being reduced to slavery or fleeing to Russia.

29. M. Sanjdorj, *Manchu Chinese Colonial Rule in Northern Mongolia*, London, C. Hurst, 1980, pp. 25 et seq.

30. Mu Ch'ien, *Traditional Government in Imperial China. A Critical Analysis*, Hong Kong, Chinese University Press, 1982, p. 133.

31. Abbé Grosier, *Description générale de la Chine*, Paris, 1787, vol. 1, p. 236. (This translation from *A General Description of China*, London, 1788, vol. I, p. 218.)

32. Lombard-Salmon, *Un exemple d'acculturation chinoise*, p. 201.

33. Quoted in ibid., p. 159.

34. Djang Chu Wen, *The Moslem Rebellion*, p. 177. While this was the dominant position and guided the government's policy, different viewpoints did exist, expressed by Li Hongzhang, governor-general of Zhili:

   Besides the difficulties involved in the original military conquest, since the seizure of Sinkiang, from the time of Ch'ien-lung, every year we need to spend three million or more taels for military expenses there even in peacetime. It is poor economics to gain several thousand *li* of wild territory, thus increasing a financial burden for thousands of years. Furthermore, the land adjoins Russia on the north, with various Moslem countries such as Turkey, Arabia and Persia on the west; and it is close to British India in the south. The neighbors are growing stronger and stronger, while we are getting weaker and weaker... Even if we do barely recover the land, we will never be able to keep it long. I read in foreign newspapers and receive other information from the west, that the Moslem chief in Kashgar [Yacub Beg] has recently received Turkey's protection and also concluded commercial treaties with Great Britain and Russia. That means he has already linked up with the various powers... Judging by this situation, both... Russia... and Great Britain will not like to see China's success in the west. Considering our own strength, it is really not enough to protect the western frontier... Tseng Kuo-fan once suggested giving up the area west of Chia-yü-kuan [Guansu] for the time being, so that we can concentrate our strength on suppressing the rebels inside the Great Wall. It was really a piece of wise, experienced, loyal advice... May I suggest that Your Majesty order all the commanders to stay strictly inside the present front line, and use their soldiers for farming instead of marching forward. At the same time, the government should appease those Moslem chiefs in Ili, Urumchi and Kashgar and permit them to have their own state as long as they will nominally use our calendar [=accept our sovereignty] ... Besides, even if Sinkiang should not be recovered, it will not hurt the whole nation. On the contrary, if we do not defend the coast, the danger will directly threaten the heart of the country ... To take care of both the long coast line in the southeast and the long supply line in the northwest is simply impossible (quoted by Djang Chu Wen, *The Moslem Rebellion*, pp. 166–7).

35.   Ibid., pp. 191 et seq.
36.   Tse-Tsung Chow, 'The May Fourth Movement', in *Harvard East Asian Studies VI*, Harvard University Press.
37.   Sun Yat Sen, *San Min Chu I. The Three Principles of the People*, tr. Frank W. Price and ed. L. T. Chen, Shanghai, 1930.
38.   Quoted in *Notes et Études Documentaires. Les Minorités ethniques de la Chine continentale*, 27 February 1960, no. 2639, p. 6.
39.   Harold Isaacs, *The Tragedy of the Chinese Revolution*, 2nd rev. ed., Stanford, Stanford University Press, 1971.
40.   On the national question and the debates within social-democracy: Georges Haupt, Michael Lowy, Claudie Weil, *Les Marxistes et la question nationale (1848–1914)*, Paris, Maspero, 1974.
      Georges Haupt, 'Dynamisme et conservatisme de l'idéologie: Rosa Luxemburg à l'orée de la recherche marxiste dans le domaine national', in *Pluriel*, no. 11, 1975, pp. 3–37.
42.   On this question see Stalin's pamphlet, said to have been written by Lenin, *Marxism and the National Question*, New York, International, 1942.
43.   Leon Trotsky, *Entre l'Impérialisme et la Révolution*, Brussels, La Taupe, 1970, p. 159.
44.   Quoted by C. Brandt, B. Schwarz and J. K. Fairbanks, *A Documentary History of Chinese Communism*, New York, Atheneum, 1966, p. 223.

45. The VII congress of the Comintern proposed a truce and an anti-Japanese alliance (July—August 1935) and renewed its pressure after the signing of the Anti-Comintern Pact between Japan and Germany in September 1936.

46. Quoted in *Notes et Etudes Documentaires*.

47. It is striking to compare this position to the attitude of the French Communist Party which, for the sake of the Popular Front, stopped using the slogan of independence for Indochina.

48. Feng Wang (Commissar for Nationalities), 'A great victory in our minorities policy', in *People's Daily*, 1 October 1951.

49. Yong Kang Zhen, *A brilliant future for the development of the languages of the national minorities*, 1st session of the People's National Assembly, 11 February 1958, quoted by R. Poulin, 'La politique de sinisation des nationalités minoritaires en RPC', in *Pluriel*, no. 25, 1981, p. 65.

50. Mao Zedong, 'The Debate on the Co-operative Transformation of Agriculture and the Current Class Struggle' (11 October 1955), in *Selected Works of Mao Tsetung*, vol. V, Peking, Foreign Languages Press, 1977, p. 230, and 'On the Ten Major Relationships' (25 August 1954), ibid., pp. 295—6.

51. Feng Wang, *On the rectification campaign and socialist education among National Minorities*, Hsinhua News Agency, no. 106, Wednesday, 5 March 1958.

52. June Teufel-Breyer, 'China's Quest for a Socialist Solution', in *Problems of Communism*, Sept.—Oct. 1975, vol. XXIV.

53. R. Macfarquhar, *The Hundred Flowers Campaign and the Chinese Intellectuals*, New York, Praeger, 1960, p. 255.

54. On Chinese policy in Xinjiang, see: Denise Helly, 'Mouvements nationalitaires en RPC. Le cas des Musulmans du Xinjiang (1949—1963)', in *Pluriel*, no. 32-3, 1983, pp. 85-100. For Tibet: 'What the second delegation saw in Tibet', in *Tibetan Review*, New Delhi, no. 9, September 1980. On the Zhuang: Richard Poulin, 'La politique de sinisation des nationalités minoritaires en RPC', in *Pluriel*, no. 25, 1981, pp. 75 et seq.

55. La Documentation Française, *Les Minorités nationales en RPC*, no. 146, 20 October 1972.

56. Fei Hsiao Tung, 'Ethnic Identification in China', in *Toward a People's Anthropology*, Peking, New World Press, 1981, p. 62.

57. Lao Zi, *Tao Te Ching*, tr. D. C. Lau, in *Chinese Classics*, Hong Kong, Chinese University Press, 1963, Book One, II.

58. *Dispute sur le sel et le fer. Yantie Lun*, tr. D. Weulersse, J. Levi and P. Baudry, Paris, Lanzmann et Seghers, pp. 201-2.

59. Ibid., p. 231.

60. Address on the seventeenth anniversary of the foundation of the People's Republic of China (1 October 1966), in M. Ebon, *Lin Piao, the Life and Writings of China's New Leader*, New York, Stein and Day, 1970, p. 280.

5

The Soviet Response
to the Minority Problem

RENÉ TANGAC

Soviet 'nationality policy' often has a bad press: the crushing of the central Asian revolts in the 1920s and 1930s, the deportation to Asia of whole peoples during the war,[1] the repeated refusal to grant the Crimean Tatars the right to return, religious persecution notably against Christian minorities[2] — these have left a disastrous impression.

This reputation has meant that the rights guaranteed (in theory) by the present constitution and those that preceded it to the 49 per cent of the USSR's population who are members of minorities,[3] the economic and social progress of the Caucasian and Asian union republics and the development of *national* cultures begun in the 1920s have been generally underestimated.

In fact, leaving aside certain constitutional provisos that empty Soviet nationality policy of any meaning, and a number of governmental, cultural or social practices that restrain national particularisms, the USSR's response to the minority problem has much that deserves attention. The fruit of long reflection, it has been applied systematically and tenaciously, and has the merit of being all-embracing, structured and well-formulated. It constitutes a not insignificant contribution to the resolution anywhere of 'the national question'.[4]

It is therefore well worth answering the following questions: what is the *background, history and spirit* of Soviet nationality policy? what is its *content* in the present context of the USSR? and what are its *results and limitations*?

Finally, we may ask how far such a policy could serve as a *model* — at least a theoretical one — outside the socialist world where, it has to be said, the various ways in which the model has been implemented have been rather distorted.

Background: The Bolsheviks and the National Question, from Revolutionary Theory to the Government of the USSR

[T]he Tsarist effort to cope with the nationality problems... emphasized stubborn Russification, suppression, and the divide-and-rule strategy of deliberately provoking national, racial and religious antagonisms. While the stress on Great Russian nationalism was intended to, and in a measure did, build support for the autocracy among the people of the dominant nationality, the reaction among other nationalities, particularly in the borderlands, was only to kindle separatist aspirations and to unleash centrifugal tendencies which threatened the disintegration of the Empire.[5]

Even if this quotation from Merle Fainsod is too hard on tsarist rule and 'Great Russian nationalism', which was capable of a degree of flexibility towards minorities, it gives an accurate picture of the 'national revolution' with which the Bolsheviks were confronted in November 1917. 'The prison of peoples' was then undergoing an upheaval that seemed to portend its rapid dissolution. In central Asia, the Karakirghiz, in revolt against conscription, had just been massacred in their tens of thousands but did not appear to be crushed; in the Caucasus, Georgia was asserting its revolutionary distinctiveness by adopting the Menshevik line; in the west, the Ukraine and Lithuania had already proclaimed their independence; as for the grand-duchy of Finland in the north, it too was trying to gain autonomy and was expecting official recognition by the new Soviet government.

As chairman of the Council of People's Commissars, Lenin appointed as Commissar for Nationalities the Georgian revolutionary Josif Vissarionovich Dzhugashvili, who had made his mark in 1913 with an article in the Bolshevik journal *Prosveschcheniye*[6] entitled 'Marxism and Social-Democracy' and signed with the pseudonym 'Stalin'. This article, written at Lenin's request and inspired by him, provided the theoretical bases of a nationality policy from which the Soviet communists were scarcely ever — at least apparently — to stray.

It is important to note first of all that this fundamental approach was already the fruit of reflection on the crises that had torn the party: it demonstrated a *compromise between the revolution's use of the 'national question' and the refusal to split the party, and ultimately the Soviet state, because of this question.*

Already in the pre-revolutionary period, the Bolsheviks had closely examined the nationality problem. They were concerned to use discontent among the minorities against the tsarist autocracy while at the same time preventing the party from disintegrating into national groups. This had already happened when the Bund, the Jewish revolutionary organization, had asserted its independence in 1898 because the party congress had refused to recognize it as 'the sole representative of the Jewish proletariat in whatever region of Russia it resided'. It is easy to imagine the embarrassment felt by the Bolshevik theoreticians: they had brandished the right to secession to win over the minorities while refusing, in the name of centralism, to divide the revolutionary movement.

Such was the contradiction that Lenin asked Stalin to overcome — or gloss over — in the article he suggested he write. A reading of this essay, which cleverly linked nationality to the colonial question, shows that the Georgian managed the situation very well.

Stalin's 1913 theses were truly revolutionary to the extent that, unlike the previous imperial policy which aimed to Russify the populations, they suggested recognition of the diversity of these populations. The starting point of the reasoning was the following: '*A nation is a historically constituted, stable community of people, formed on the basis of a common language, territory, economic life, and psychological make-up manifested in a common culture.*'[7] History, language, territory, economy and a common culture are the five 'Stalinist categories' that acted as criteria in the 1920s and 1930s to designate, and in some cases to form, national entities.

But Stalin, an advocate of diversification, did not extend such freedom to the party. His theses were endorsed a few months after their publication in a five-point resolution of the Bolshevik central committee which summarizes the meaning and reservations of the new theoretical approach:

1. a democratic republic with complete equality of rights for all nationalities and languages, public education in the local language and to a large extent local autonomy;
2. rejection of the Austrian principle of 'cultural autonomy' extended to the whole country;
3. rejection of any division of the labour movement by nationalities;
4. the right for all the nations of the tsarist empire to self-determination, defined as the right to secession and formation of an independent state;
5. finally this right does not prejudice the appropriateness of the measure itself.[8]

It was on the basis of this last point that the Bolsheviks were endlessly

to split hairs. Stalin himself had already opened up this prospect in
1913:

> The Transcaucasian Tatars as a nation may assemble, let us say, in their
> diet and, succumbing to the influence of their beys and mullahs, decide
> to restore the old order of things and to secede from the state ... But
> will this be in the interest of the toiling strata of the Tatar nation? Can
> Social-Democracy look on indifferently when the beys and mullahs
> assume the leadership of the masses in the solution of the national
> question? Should not Social-Democracy interfere in the matter?[9]

In May 1918, after six months at the Commissariat of Nationalities,
Stalin replied to his own question:

> Autonomy is a form. The whole question is what class content is put
> into this form. The Soviet power is not at all opposed to autonomy. It
> is in favour of autonomy, but only such autonomy in which the entire
> power belongs to the workers and peasants, and in which the bourgeois
> of all nationalities are debarred not only from power, but even from
> participation in the election of government bodies.[10]

In other words, the Commissar for Nationalities of the Bolshevik
government only accepted national autonomy to the extent that it served
the revolution and was controlled by it. We have already come a long way
from the independence granted to Finland (but in the hope of a revolution) in 1917. It is true that the accusations of auctioning Russia, the
Treaty of Brest-Litovsk and the horror of war communism [*communisme
de guerre*], had obliterated theory in the face of overwhelming realities.
Lenin himself admitted that 'the right to self-determination is one thing,
while the appropriateness of separation for this or that nation is something
else.'[11]
    In order to avoid this embarrassing choice, Lenin conceived in 1918 of
a new power to be attributed to the revolution: the power to bring the
nationalities together. 'The example of the Russian Soviet republic shows
that the federation we are building will be a step towards the unity of the
different nationalities of Russia, in a single democratic and centralized
Soviet state.'[12] Such a move towards unity prefigured the '*Sblijenie*'
(drawing together) and *Sliyanie* (fusion) so dear to Khrushchev, Brezhnev
and Andropov.
    Starting from these theoretical premises, there ensued at the highest
echelons of power a strange duet between the Russian Lenin, who was
increasingly aware of the dangers of Great Russian chauvinism,[13] and the

Georgian Stalin, who was dedicated to re-establishing the complete authority of the central government by making the Russian republic the core of the federation.

Despite his fears, however, Lenin, removed from affairs by illness, allowed Stalin to carry out — among other activities — his national policy. The Commissar for Nationalities had little difficulty in drawing together the threads of policy in the remote republics: as Commissar of Workers' and Peasants' Inspection as well, he had complete control of appointments and dismissals. The shortage of cadres enabled him to appoint men loyal to him.

Under these conditions the creation of socialist republics followed the advance of the Red Army and they were modelled on the RSFSR (Russian Soviet Federative Socialist Republic). In November 1918 the republic of the Ukraine was founded, and in February 1919 that of Byelorussia. In June 1919 these republics accepted a sort of 'workers and peasants' union' with the RSFSR covering all the key attributes of power: army, war economy, finance, railways. In the Caucasus, where the Menshevik Georgian republic was crushed in 1921, the process took longer and was more all-embracing: Azerbaijan, Armenia and Georgia were brought together in 1922 in a Transcaucasian republic which survived until 1936.

From the very beginning, the institutions of the RSFSR thus had authority over some activities in the other republics. This was the case with the Red Army, to which the armed forces of the republics were attached, and with a number of economic services. But the control by the 'centre' remained discreet.

The year 1922 saw an effort by Stalin to promote the legal framework of the 'federal system' vaguely envisaged by the Bolsheviks. His theses on 'autonomization' envisaged the republics adhering to the RSFSR within which they would enjoy a status of autonomy (and not sovereignty). Meeting with opposition from Lenin and the new republic of Georgia, this 'Great Russian chauvinist' proposal was withdrawn. But Stalin manoeuvred. Aware of the distortion that would inevitably emerge between *law* (the equality of nations) and *fact* (control by the centre through economic organs, the army and especially the party), the Commissar for Nationalities gave up the idea of autonomization and drew up a new proposal in conformity with Lenin's ideas.

This proposal, accepted by the Pact of September 1922 and repeated in the 1924 and 1936 constitutions, still figures virtually intact in the 1977 constitution. It will be enough then to examine this constitution to illustrate the rejection of national opposition and the will for diversification (divide and rule), that mark the spirit of 'socialist federalism'.[14] To this we will add some thoughts about the present statutes of the

Soviet Communist Party that are essential for understanding the homeland of the dictatorship of the proletariat.

Content of the Nationality Policy: From the Appearance of Equality to the Pre-eminence of a Russian State Tradition

The Soviet constitution of October 1977 stresses the cohesion of the Soviet people. In it the state is described as 'a socialist state of the whole people'[15] which has 'put an end once and for all to ... strife between nationalities'. The Soviet people is 'a new historical community of people' formed 'on the basis of the drawing together of all classes and social strata, and of the juridical and factual equality of all its nations and nationalities, on their fraternal co-operation'.

The supreme goal of the Soviet state is 'the building of a classless communist society in which there will be public, communist self government'. To this end, various main aims are indicated. Three concern us here: 'to lay the material and technical foundation of communism, to perfect socialist social relations and transform them into communist relations, to mould the citizen of communist society'.[16]

What must be grasped about the communist project for the minorities is that it is an integral part of the determination to transform society totally. New relations have to be defined; a new man, 'homo sovieticus', who has overcome national particularisms, egoisms and 'chauvinisms', has to be moulded. All nationalities, including the Russians, must go through this process. Thus in theory all peoples are treated equally. Since the goal aimed at is seen as good, and the enterprise embarked on follows the inevitable course of history, 'the socialist state of the whole people' is seen as 'expressing the will and interests of the workers, peasants, and intelligentsia, the working people of all the nations and nationalities of the country'.[17]

Thus the theory of the Stalinist categories mentioned above was translated into the creation of a 'federative structure' which, at different levels, gives a state and communist party structure to at least 53 Soviet nationalities.[18] This impressive administrative reality is worth consideration.

The highest stage is that of the *union republic*, which is theoretically a sovereign state. Fifteen nations — including the Russian one — are felt to meet the requirement of the five categories of history, language, territory, economy and culture. But other concerns come into play. The Finno-Karelians, for example, lost their union republic in 1936 for an autonomous republic probably because it was judged to be too dangerous for the Soviet Finns to live next door to then anti-communist Finland.

It should be noted on this point that all the union republics are situated on the periphery of the RSFSR and have an international frontier: that would seem to indicate the original concern to use the national specificity of these republics for external purposes, for the revolution.

The second stage of recognition of a nation is that of the *autonomous republic*, whose state framework is not sovereign. This category comprises smaller nations or ones that do not meet the requirements of the five categories. It is applied mainly to peoples living well inside the country's borders and having no international frontiers. Among the 20 autonomous republics, apart from the special case of Karelia and the altogether illusory international frontier of Buratia and Tuva with a People's Republic of Mongolia (which has no real independence), only tiny Nakhichevan has an international frontier, with Iran. As for the autonomous republic of Tartaria, its inclusion within Russia seems to have been a pretext for maintaining as an autonomous republic a feared nation[19] that fulfilled the requirements of the five categories.

Finally, for the 'nationalities' — that is, for ethnic groups that are too little developed to aspire to the rank of a nation — there exists the stage of *autonomous regions* and *autonomous areas*. This status guarantees to tiny minorities (sometimes numbering only a few thousand) their own cultural rights, together with special social assistance. There are ten autonomous areas and eight autonomous regions. We might note in passing the predictable failure of the autonomous region of Birobidjan, a territory in the Siberian far east allotted to Jews.

This federal organization is complemented by a constitutional law which, at least in some of its articles, appears to ensure the protection of cultural peculiarities. Article 34 lays down, for example, that: 'Citizens of the USSR are equal before the law, without distinction of origin, social or property status, race or nationality, sex, education, language, attitude to religion, type and nature of occupation, domicile or other status.' Article 36 is even more explicit:

Citizens of the USSR of different races and nationalities have equal rights.

Exercise of these rights is ensured by a policy of all-round development and drawing together of all the nations and nationalities of the USSR, by educating citizens in the spirit of Soviet patriotism and socialist internationalism, and by the possibility to use their native language and the languages of other peoples of the USSR.

Any direct or indirect limitation of the rights of citizens or establishment of direct or indirect privileges on grounds of race or nationality, and any advocacy of racial or national exclusiveness, hostility or contempt, are punishable by law.

Faced with this impressive 'declaration of intent', the problem is now to understand how the Soviet government invokes the constitution to allow it *de facto* control of nations and nationalities in the face of the guarantees and institutions that are *de jure* guaranteed them.

According to the constitution the integral, federal multinational state[20] is a 'voluntary association of equal Soviet Socialist Republics'. Each of the union republics, the living framework and the symbol of the sovereignty of the large nationalities (15 today), has the right to secede from the USSR.[21] 'A sovereign Soviet Socialist state ... exercises independent authority on its territory' and 'has its own constitution.'[22] It 'has the right to enter into relations with other states . . .'[23]

But a formal infringement of the equality of the union republics should be noted: among these 'republics equal in law', only the Russian Soviet Federative Socialist Republic adds the qualifier 'federative' to the usual name. This is not accidental since, in the institutions of the USSR, this republic federates the others; it is, in Orwell's words, 'more equal than the others'. The RSFSR, it must not be forgotten, embraces 76 per cent of the territory of the USSR and 53 per cent of the Soviet people; it incorporates 16 of the 20 autonomous republics, five of the eight autonomous regions and all the autonomous areas. The result is that there is a considerable overlap between the composition of the supreme soviet of the USSR and that of the RSFSR. But, as we shall see, at the vital level of the Communist Party, the identity is total since fusion between the USSR and RSFSR was achieved in that area in 1966. Given that fact, and knowing that the Russian language is the language of the state, the Russian republic clearly has a considerable weight and exercises an almost inevitable domination within the federation.

Another infringement of the sovereign power of the union republics flows from article 73 — the longest one in the whole constitution — which sets out the full extent of central powers. The purpose of this text which, significantly, immediately follows the article granting the right of secession, is, it seems, to take back for the USSR everything in the rest of the constitution tending to strengthen the sovereignty of the union republics.

It does so in twelve points stressing the competence of the Soviet Union 'in the person of the highest bodies of state authority and administration' for:

1) the admission of new republics (point 1);[24]
2) the determination of state boundaries (point 2);
3) the general principles of the administrative and legislative organization of the USSR and the republics (points 3 and 4);
4) the pursuance of a uniform social and economic policy: direction, planning, budget (points 5, 6 and 7);

5) defence problems (point 8);
6) state security, the notorious KGB (point 9);
7) foreign affairs (point 10);
8) control over the observance of the constitution (point 11).

For good measure, point 12 — which is very vague — gives Moscow 'the settlement of other matters of All-Union importance'. As if that were not enough, article 74 gives union law primacy over the law of the republics. Finally, article 75 reiterates that the USSR 'comprises the territory of the Union Republics'.

In order to grasp clearly the nature of the balance between the central government and the union republics, let us take the example of foreign affairs. Article 80 (already cited in part)[25] asserts the autonomy of the union republics: 'A Union Republic has the right to enter into relations with other states, conclude treaties with them, exchange diplomatic and consular representatives, and take part in the work of international organisations.' Yet point 10 of article 73 gives almost all the real power to central government. It is responsible for:

Representation of the USSR in international relations; the USSR's relations with other states and with international organisations; *establishment of the general procedure for, and co-ordination of, the relations of the Union Republics with other states and international organisations*; foreign trade and other forms of external economic activity on the basis of state monopoly [emphasis added].

This balance between central and regional powers is reflected in the union republics in the existence of a ministry of foreign affairs purely for purposes of representation and protocol. The representatives of Byelorussia at the UN obviously have no room for manoeuvre *vis-à-vis* the delegation of the USSR. At most there have been simply a few consular agreements signed by Western and Eastern countries with the Ukraine.

Under these conditions, 'the highest bodies of state authority and administration'[26] — the Council of Ministers, the ministries and the state committees — exercise tight control from Moscow over the nations and nationalities.

This control takes two main forms. First, the Council of Ministers of the USSR has 'the right, in matters within the jurisdiction of the Union of Soviet Socialist Republics, to suspend execution of decisions and ordinances of the Councils of Ministers of Union Republics...' Secondly, under the constitution, the principal ministries of a union republic (called union-republican ministries) and its state committees 'shall be subordinate to both the Council of Ministers of the Union Republic and the corresponding Union-Republican ministry or State Committee of the USSR'.[28] That means that the central government has a right of oversight and veto over such key administrations as those of the ministries of the interior, education, justice, finance and agriculture. The same is true with such a basic part of the system as the Committee of State Security (the KGB), and responsibility for defence, which figured since 1945 in the organizational chart of the union republics, returned to the union in 1977.

So what power do the union republics still have? Mainly regional and local administration, defined by the list of so-called republican ministries: consumer services, municipal services, social security, roads and local transport. Many people from other nationalities work in these areas of activity but rarely appear in any government hierarchy with major responsibilities. They are especially scarce in key ministries, the army in particular.[29]

Such discrimination hardly reflects the letter of article 36 cited above. So to keep up the appearance of federalism, nationals are appointed in the hierarchy of the republics — and even in the federal hierarchy — to all honorific positions without real power.

In the final analysis, the harsh grip of the government and the state administration on the minorities — but also on the Russian majority — is maintained while always respecting a two-faced constitution. While freedom is asserted in some articles (and taken up by propaganda), others remove it. On this point, let us take an article that is especially sensitive for most nationalities: that covering the issue of religion. In article 52, freedom of conscience is affirmed, as is the freedom to carry on atheist propaganda. This last point provides a legal basis for an elaborate anti-religious struggle which parades 'constitutional' respect for freedom of conscience and even the maintenance of retrograde forms of worship, the better to attack and undermine religion. We shall return to this tactic below.

This gap between declared intention and reality, which is perceptible in the letter of the constitution, is also found in the rules and composition of the Communist Party. The rules envisage, for example, the existence of a communist party of each union republic like that of the CP of the USSR with its own congress, central committee, etc. But for an organization that stresses 'the monolithic cohesion of [the party's] ranks',[30] it is obvious that the 14 national parties are, just like the regional bodies of a similar level,[31] totally subordinated to the central authorities in Moscow. As no more than a public demonstration of federalism, they have no real autonomy.

The fifteenth party, that of the Russian republic, has been indistinguishable from the party of the Soviet Union since 1966. Since that date, the Politburo, the supreme body of the party, has acted as Politburo of the RSFSR. The identification of the Russian republic with the USSR and hence the influence of the Russian state tradition on the Soviet state have thus been strengthened. It matters little, therefore, that the Communist Party has four million members belonging to non-Slav minorities, representing 20 per cent of the total, for they rarely reach positions of great responsibility.

Yet the party might seem to have achieved a policy of indigenization. The nomination of the Azerbaijani Geïdar Aliev to the Political Bureau as a regular member and first vice-chairman of the Council of Ministers provides an example of federalism at the top[32] which is strengthened by the presence in the Politburo of the Kazakh Kunaev, a regular member, and the Georgian Shevardnadze, an alternate member. But these cases are deceptive. The proportion of Slavs at the top of the party is 81 per cent in the Political Bureau (13 members out of 16)[33] and 100 per cent in the secretariat (nine members). In the party itself, out of 80 per cent of Slavs, the Russians comprise 60 per cent. These percentages must, of course, be compared to the proportion of Slavs and Russians in the country (71 and 51 per cent respectively). The gap is in fact even greater because the non-Russians often hold the lowest posts, leaving senior positions to others. It is true that to give an appearance of federalism, a first secretary belonging to the local nationality is often appointed to the head of the Communist Party of a republic. But he is assisted by a second secretary who is almost always a Slav and very often a Russian and who is in a position to control his hierarchical superior. The First Secretary, an outsider of proven loyalty to the Soviet system, is not altogether powerless. But, reduced to a role of representation, he has to delegate his numerous responsibilities.[34] Being in addition closely 'assisted', he has to observe perfect orthodoxy.

How can we judge and understand this present-day organization of the nationality policy? Its forerunners in the Soviet constitutions of 1924 and 1936[35] showed an even wider gap between the generosity of the legal text and the petty interference — indeed, the harshness — of its application: thus Stalin intended to cultivate the appearance of law in order to better hide his despotism. In these conditions of authoritarianism, the Russian state tradition was soon strengthened, at the time of the war, by the appeal to Russian patriotism. This trend became all the more entrenched as some minorities, feeling little loyalty to the Soviet government during the conflict, had less confidence than ever in the Kremlin. Despite the grandiloquent speeches of Khrushchev, Brezhnev and Andropov on friendship among peoples and their 'drawing together' and 'fusion', this mistrust has persisted; the repatriation to the USSR in 1980 of Soviet soldiers of

Muslim origin serving in Afghanistan is a recent illustration of the persistent mistrust. The amending of the existing constitution in 1977 was another sign. We have shown its skilfully contradictory, two-faced character and the fact that it is much less federal in spirit than the constitution of 1936. It has the advantage over its predecessor, however, of being much less hypocritically applied.

Application of the Nationality Policy: From Favourable Appearances to Deceptive Realities

The minorities' toil and skill, the riches of their territories, and a system which has promoted the development of the Soviet Union as a whole have made Tashkent, Tbilissi and Tallin into cities that have little need to envy Moscow. Sometimes even the countryside of central Asia, Transcaucasia and, *a fortiori*, the Baltic republics is more prosperous and more developed than the Russian and Byelorussian homeland.

Can one then reasonably speak of colonization? Of course, the Soviet army stationed in the non-Slav areas is almost entirely Slav; of course, the peasants who came from European Russia expropriated Kazakh shepherds; inevitably, the cities of central Asia have their Slav elite, their European areas and their native quarters. But it is still the case that Russian colonization is not like the usual model: it is certainly less guilty of exploitation than other colonial systems.

Let us take the example of central Asia. Here the Slavs (even in imperial Russia) brought modernity, the right to life and some improvement in the status of women in the five union republics in this region. Everything is not perfect, especially in terms of real autonomy. But these territories, which in the last century were on the level of Afghanistan, are much more developed than all the countries of central and eastern continental Asia. The 'pax Sovietica' prevails there;[36] the cultural heritage (notably the linguistic and artistic heritage) appears to have been preserved; the population, despite its considerable growth, enjoys a reasonable standard of living.

In fact, to give a balanced appreciation, it is important to take account of the less glossy aspects of Soviet nationality policy and its central aim. This aim does not involve promoting respect for minorities, their authenticity or their law. It is a question, according to a quotation from Lenin used by Andropov,[37] of ensuring not only the drawing together of nations but also their fusion (*Sliyanie*). The result has been different policies varying in their emphasis but all directed to this end. The main strands of these policies were:

• the far-sighted and generous policies of the 1920s and early 1930s in line with 'Stalinist diversification', which included the promotion of vernacular languages, literacy campaigns, modernization of societies, ethnological research and medical and social aid to the most disadvantaged minorities;[38]

• the strong-arm method: the crushing of the Basmachi guerillas in the 1920s and the massive deportation of 'saboteurs', notably to Kazakhstan, in the 1930s;

• the melting-pot of adversity, and trials and tribulations of all sorts ('dekulakization', agrarian reform, deportations, war, etc.) which drew peoples together by force, with none being spared, including the Russian people.

Today a more subtle policy is pursued. Let us take the example of religion. Open persecution in the manner of the 1930s is out, and the Soviet government now proclaims its tolerance. In reality, religion and the faithful are closely watched, and proselytism is forbidden. But rather than attacking the believers, it is the beliefs themselves that are attacked. These are analysed by the *'religioviedy'* (scholars of religion) as relicts of the past. Efforts are made to make them a concern of old people and to confine them to the most antiquated and obtuse tradition. The goal is to bring about a situation in which they mark time, lose their appeal and militantism, and gradually lose their symbolism and national significance. As for religious events, the policy is to restrict them and to replace them by a secular ceremonial (marriage palaces, transformation of the 'Nauruz' or Muslim new year into the peasants' spring festival, etc.) and, at all events, to keep quiet about them. Finally, whereas religious publications are extremely rare, those of the Association for the Propagation of Political and Scientific Knowledge are plentiful and varied.

In short, each people, according to the Soviet theory of gradual erosion of particularisms and of a gradual day-by-day Sovietization, is felt to become more and more part of a whole which, according to the same process, will spread to the whole socialist world. In his speech on the sixtieth anniversary of the USSR on 20 December 1982, Yuri Andropov outlined the actions to be taken:[39] first of all promoting economic integration and better communications between the republics; encouraging — notably through radio and television — a 'mutual enrichment of cultures'; and finally, struggling against every form of 'pride and vanity'.

According to Andropov, this transformation will be achieved through better propaganda, increased vigilance by the party and a renewed appeal to action by the Komsomol, the trade unions and the army. It will also be necessary that 'all the nationalities living in any particular republic be duly represented in the various aspects of the organs of the party and the USSR'. Thus 'national differences' — which, as Andropov admitted, will last much longer than class differences — should be attenuated.

Yet this recourse to classical remedies, with action deferred to some later date, has produced results, notably in the autonomous republics, which have been less able than the union republics to sidestep directives from Moscow. Cultural and religious uprooting is advancing everywhere at the slow tempo of a Sovietization which in many respects is simply Russification. The minorities, often pitted against one another by the system,[40] continue to be jealous of one another. The 'show-case effect' organized for each foreign delegation that is taken through the fine federal capitals (Tashkent, Tallin, Alma-Ata, etc.) often deprives the nationalities of the USSR of obvious reasons for being pitied and supported by the outside world.

The upshot for these minorities is neither a renunciation of their existence nor a suicidal revolt. No doubt the minorities have learned from decades of trials and tribulations; faced with the Soviet enterprise, they have lapsed into a sort of undeclared passive resistance.

This resistance may take various disguises, from demographic growth (a sort of 'revenge of the cradles') to legal resistance (that of the Tatars) by way of the defence of the ancestral heritage against attacks by Soviet culture ('Mirasism').

It should be noted that the union republics seem better able to allow Mirasism and legal resistance than the autonomous republics. In the latter, a real eradication of traditions seems to be occurring in a process facilitated by the numerical and cultural weakness of the small minorities. Conversely, the union republics have a potential defence against Russification: constitutional guarantees, administrative inertia and cultural vigour enable them to keep alive the national spirit. It still remains true that the traditional grip of the Russian majority and the centralizing imperatives of the Soviet system infringe on even the letter of the constitution and on the rights 'guaranteed' to minorities. But in the end, despite all the subterfuges, the constitution of the USSR and those of the union republics do not operate only in favour of the central government.

Notes

1. Crimea Tatars, Volga Germans, Kalmuks, Chechens, Ingushes, Ossets, Meskhet Turks, etc.
2. Catholics of Lithuania or sub-Carpathian Ukraine, Uniates, Baptists, etc.
3. Alongside 59 per cent of Russians (143 million) there are 20 per cent of Ukrainian and Byelorussian Slavs (56 million), 20 per cent of Turkish- or Farsi-speaking Muslims. The remaining 9 per cent (25 million) are divided into over 70 ethnic groups (Caucasians, Balts, Siberians, etc.).
4. The traditional name in the Russian empire for the minority problem.

5. Merle Fainsod, *How Russia is Governed*, Cambridge (Mass.), Harvard University Press.
6. Russian word meaning 'teaching'.
7. Stalin, *Prosveschcheniye*, no. 3–5, March 1913, Moscow, *Works*, vol. 2, Moscow, Foreign Languages Publishing House, 1953, pp. 300–81.
8. 'The Communist Party ... in the resolutions and decisions of the Congresses', vol. I, *Partizdat*, 1932, pp. 238–40 (in Russian).
9. Stalin, 'The National Question and Social-Democracy', in *Works*, vol. 2, p. 323.
10. Stalin, *Works*, vol. 4, p. 89.
11. Lenin, *Works*, vol. 19, p. 476.
12. Quoted by H. Carrère d'Encausse, *Decline of an Empire: The Soviet Socialist Republics in Revolt*, New York, Newsweek Books, 1979.
13. Cf. Lenin, 'Scratch some Communists and you will find Great-Russian chauvinists', speech closing the debate on the party programme, 19 March 1919, *Collected Works*, vol. 29, p. 194.
14. Article 70 of the constitution.
15. Preamble to the constitution.
16. Preamble to the constitution.
17. Article 1 (author's emphasis).
18. In fact many more since administrative units such as the autonomous republic of Daghestan (in the Caucasus) or the autonomous region of Gorno-Altai (in continental Asia) include several nationalities.
19. In the eyes of the Russians, the Tatars bear the responsibility for the occupation they suffered from the thirteenth to the fifteenth century: the famous 'Tatar yoke'. In the nineteenth century the Volga Tatars witnessed a renewal of Islam. Finally, a Marxist Tatar, Sultan Galiev, was the author in the 1920s of an interesting approach to the nationality policy rejected by Stalin (cf. Helène Carrère d'Encausse, *Réforme et révolution chez les Musulmans de l'Empire russe*, Paris, Armand Colin, 1966).
20. Article 70 of the 1977 Soviet constitution.
21. Article 72 of the constitution.
22. Article 76 of the constitution.
23. Article 80 of the constitution.
24. Because of the tradition of world revolution, these new republics may be chosen outside the USSR. Bulgaria or Mongolia have been spoken of as the sixteenth republic.
25. This article was added in 1945 to the 1936 constitution to give the Ukraine and Byelorussia a status enabling them to participate in the work of the UN. Another article — adopted for the same reason in 1945 but never implemented — envisaged the existence of armed forces attached to the union republics; it was removed in the 1977 constitution.
26. Article 73 of the constitution.
27. Article 134 of the constitution.
28. Article 142 of the constitution.
29. Only the KGB seems sometimes to implement a policy of indigenization by appointing nationals to its top positions in the union republics. These nationals, it is true, must already, in such a body, have given every proof of loyalty.
30. Preamble to the rules of the Communist Party.
31. Party organizations of the Oblast or the Kraï (large subdivisions of the RSFSR).
32. Sought especially by Andropov who appointed Aliev.

33. Situation in March 1985.
34. In terms of the scope of their powers, the regional or republican secretaries have been compared to the prefects of French departments.
35. What was, in the opinion of lawyers, the most federal and most democratic of constitutions inaugurated the era of the purges.
36. Since the late 1930s.
37. *Krasnaya Zvezda* of 22 December 1982, p. 2 (speech on the occasion of the sixtieth anniversary of the creation of the USSR partly devoted to the nationalities problem).
38. Notably to the peoples of Siberia.
39. Chernenko, who seemed to be implementing his predecessor's policy but with more severity, never defined his own nationality policy.
40. The constitution, for example, gives the union republics a right of oversight over their autonomous republics that is analogous to that of the union government over the union republics. In other words, the Kara-Kalpaks are to the Uzbeks what the Uzbeks are to the central government.

Part II

6

On the Notion of Diaspora

RICHARD MARIENSTRAS

A few years ago, the linguistic and economic conflicts dividing Belgium focused attention on the difficulty of guaranteeing the cultural autonomy of populations that are not the majority in the area they occupy. These conflicts had a history. Following the 1830 revolution, the monolingualism enshrined in the constitution was felt as a form of cultural oppression by Flemish-speakers. The French-speakers opposed universal bilingualism, and so a linguistic frontier was drawn in 1932; Flanders and Wallonia were each declared homogeneous, and Brussels remained a bilingual region. It was thus where one lived that officially determined to which language group one belonged and hence where schools teaching French or Flemish existed. A periodic census would modify this 'ius soli' so as to follow linguistic changes as closely as possible. However, the Brussels region was spreading at the expense of Flemish Brabant. In 1963, the Walloons, who perceived this as systematic Frenchification, succeeded in ensuring that the capital was 'frozen', that is, that it was limited to 19 communes. Since the census had been suppressed at liberation, moreover, the French-speakers of Brussels saw, so to speak, their 'linguistic soil' slide from under their feet as more and more of them began to find themselves on Flemish soil. This led to the creation of the Democratic Front of French-speakers, which called for the territory of the capital to be fixed democratically through a referendum.

At the same time, Wallonia was suffering severely from steel and coal crises, while Flanders was prospering and developing its commercial and industrial power. This situation led to the appearance of a double and contradictory federalist demand which resulted, after many ups and downs, in the 1977 'quadripartite' pact. This agreement involved both an economic programme and a pact between the communities. The French-speakers demanded regionalization, the Dutch-speakers requested new institutions created on the basis of the two linguistic communities. We are not concerned here with the details of the complicated compromise that the negotiators reached. What interests us is the statute that was drawn up for the French-speakers of the Brussels region: against the Dutch-speakers who demanded that the 'bilingual soil' of the capital should not go beyond the border of the 19 communes, the French-speakers wanted the rights of their minorities living beyond this border to be protected by constitutional guarantees. Parliament, however, strictly maintained the 'ius soli', but allowed the French-speakers in the outlying communes to adopt an administrative domicile in any of the 19 communes. It can be said that the 'freezing' of the bilingual zone put the French-speakers of the periphery in a 'diaspora', and that their administrative attachment to the central bilingual territory enabled them to get out of this situation symbolically and juridically.

This interpretation is, of course, somewhat metaphorical. It will be understood that the idea of 'diaspora' implies or may be held to imply the ideas of 'centre' and 'periphery'; the idea of a relationship or lack of relationship to the soil and the territory; the ideas of 'majority' and 'minority'; the ideas of a relation to the state, to a central or regional administration, to structuring institutions or associations. It also implies a degree of national, or cultural, or linguistic awareness — and that the economic situation of a 'diaspora' has some impact on its general situation. But it is only recently that this term has come to describe minority groups whose awareness of their identity is defined by a relationship, territorially discontinuous, with a group settled 'elsewhere' (for example: the Chinese diaspora, the Corsican diaspora in mainland France, etc.). Historically, the term described the dispersed Jewish communities, that is those not living in *Eretz Israel*.

'Diaspora' (from a Greek word meaning dispersion) presumes that there exists an independent or heavily populated Jewish political 'centre'. Some writers only use it to describe the communities that left *Eretz Israel* at times when such a centre did exist, that is the period of the first Temple and the second Temple as well as the period since the creation (in 1948) of the state of Israel. This term is then distinguished from 'Galut' (a Hebrew word meaning exile) which describes the communities at times when the centre did not exist (broadly speaking, the period between the destruction of the second Temple in AD 70 and the creation of the state of Israel). Diaspora implies voluntary and free migrations. 'Galut' implies that the home territory has fallen under domination, that the migrations and settlements were forced. For some commentators, the feeling of being in exile necessarily accompanies the condition of being exiled, and it is this close relationship between exile and consciousness of exile that is the singular feature of Jewish history; it is that which, over the centuries of migrations and vicissitudes, kept Jewish national consciousness alive.

For the twenty centuries that followed the destruction of the second Temple, countless Jewish thinkers attempted to give the exile a meaning, and this vast debate re-emerged in modern garb in the nineteenth and twentieth centuries at a time when nationalisms were becoming exacerbated and a good number of nation-states were being formed. The debate on the dispersion and exile linked up with that of nationalities or minorities aspiring to a state existence. The communities of the diaspora, especially the Yiddish-speaking ones of central and eastern Europe, took a stand on the right of peoples to self-determination and drew up plans and projects for liberation in which the old ideas linked up with new concepts.

It was naturally around the problem of territorialism that the polemic among the various tendencies of the Jewish liberation movements crystallized at the beginning of the twentieth century. The issue was important, since it concerned the fate of some nine million Jews then living in Europe, dispersed in a dozen countries, and two-thirds of whom at least were Yiddish-speaking. The advocates of a territorial base and state sovereignty tended to paint their situation in over-dark colours — though it was in truth very bad because of economic distress and anti-Semitism. Leo Pinsker (1821—91), for example, had in his youth supported the Enlightenment movement and advocated the assimilation of the Jews into Russian society. Following the pogroms of 1881 in southern Russia, he radically altered his opinions. In a pamphlet published in 1882, *Auto-emancipation*, he defined the Jews as a distinct ethnic entity, dispersed among hostile nations — an entity that could never be assimilated because of the prevailing anti-Semitism. The existence of a 'threshold of tolerance' meant that, even if they obtained legal equality, Jews could never grow demographically and win social and economic equality. Pinsker affirmed that each ethnic group tends to favour its own members to the detriment of the 'outsider' and, once the 'saturation point' had been reached, persecution began.

On the other hand, Pinsker sharply attacked the Jewish communities in the West (in France, England, Germany, etc.) which tended to present the dispersion of the Jews as a 'mission', or, following the traditional teachings, as a series of trials imposed by God that had to be suffered patiently and with resignation until the coming of the Messiah. His description of the spiritual impoverishment of the communities in exile is particularly striking. He compares them to sick creatures whose sickness has reached the conscience to such a degree that they feel normal despite the anomalies afflicting them. Pinsker and, following him, numerous Zionist thinkers affirm that the diaspora is a pathological mode of existence. For a human group, normal or natural existence is national and state existence. Any other mode of existence generates oppression and wretchedness. An ethnic group which has not formed itself into a state is a dangerously sick group. Others would say with the left-Zionist Ber Borochov that the Jewish communities of the diaspora are social beings who walk on their heads rather than on their feet. Unlike other peoples, among whom workers and peasants form the base of the social pyramid and are the largest section of the population, among the Jews, it is small traders, merchants, bourgeois and intellectuals who predominate, whereas workers and peasants are the smallest section of the population: the pyramid is thus turned upside down and seems to stand on its tip.

Leo Pinsker felt that it was necessary to encourage the awakening of national consciousness among all Jews, as he had observed that in Russia and Romania the desire to return to *Eretz Israel* had already manifested itself and become a political demand. For Ber Borochov, the 'return' to the national home would enable Jewish society to become normal, that is, to allow it to become once again a 'natural' social pyramid.

It will have been noted in passing that Pinsker has adopted the problematic used by many nationalist movements of the time. These movements postulated that every ethnic group had to form itself into a territorially-based state and made the nation-state a part of the natural order. But in most cases these were nationalities heavily settled on a territory and which had territorial demands as well as political, legal and cultural demands. Few doubted that these nationalities had rights and that they were potential nations.

Within most Jewish communities in central and eastern Europe, there was no doubt either that the Jews were a nation — or a 'nationality'. But within social-democracy and among the Marxist leaders, things were not seen in the same light. Marx and Engels had postulated the primacy of class over nation and any other historical category. They felt that the nation, a transitional, albeit necessary, stage in the development of capitalism, would disappear when the proletariat came to power. Marx insisted in addition on the viability of 'great' nations; these had to be supported, since they were historically necessary to the progress of humanity. And the working class should only identify itself with the nation if the national struggle has a revolutionary and progressive character. Marx and Engels thus neglected the aspirations of the small nationalities of Europe; these peoples of peasants without a bourgeoisie, or workers, or intellectuals, could not — they thought — develop a culture and political life of their own.

Another yardstick was also used: that of the 'peoples without history'. Following Hegel, Engels asserted that peoples that had never formed states in the past could not construct any viable one in the future. Marx and Engels thus stood in opposition to the theorists of the traditional European national movements, for whom every nation was a fact of nature and had the *natural right* to independence.

It was not until the end of the century that there was any broadening of these views within social-democracy. Whereas for Marx the nation was inconceivable without a nation-state that stood above legal, linguistic, territorial and cultural frontiers, article 4 of the resolution of the Brünn Congress (1899) of the Austrian Social-Democractic Party envisaged protection of the rights of minorities, which was a break with the principle of territorialism. 'Diasporas' henceforth had a theoretical right to be heard, given of course that each nationality had also to dispose of 'self-governing territories' (article 3), that is of a territorial centre.

In 1899, too, Karl Renner in his pamphlet *State and Nation* tried to reconcile the principles of territorial autonomy and personal autonomy; he wanted to organize the dispersed communities of each nationality into legal persons. And Otto Bauer, in his major work *The Question of Nationalities and Social-Democracy* (1907), distinguished three types of national communities: tribal or traditional collectivities; those based on the cultural unity of the ruling class; and those that would be endowed with autonomy in the future socialist society. Distinguishing between the community of fate (which determines national character) and the community of character or shared lot (which forms the basis of class solidarity), Bauer suggested 'national-cultural autonomy' when territorial continuity is interrupted and when minority nationalities cannot lay claim to national independence.

Bauer's views and the demand for national-cultural autonomy were later strongly attacked by Lenin and Stalin. Conversely, they were taken up by the Jewish labour movement. At its congress in 1904, the Bund demanded cultural and national autonomy for the Jews. Already in 1901, one of the resolutions of the Bund asserted that 'Russia... must become a federation of nationalities with, for each nationality, full autonomy, whatever the territory occupied... The concept of nationality must also apply to the Jewish people.'

What such a programme assumed is that a people with a history and a culture has enough claims to demand national rights, and can do so independently of whether it has a territorial base. That amounts to recognizing and legitimizing the existence of the diaspora. The positions of the Bund were challenged from various directions: by Zionist, religious or assimilationist Jewish circles; by the Bolsheviks; by the Polish Socialist Party (PPS); and, paradoxically, by Otto Bauer himself, who wrote that 'the Jews were a nation, they are no longer one... they are integrated into the nations where they live.' He also wrote that Jews are a 'nation without history', and he appealed to Jewish workers to demand no more Jewish schools but to send their children to the German, Polish or Ukrainian schools. Bauer was so insistent that in an article in which he attacked national-cultural autonomy, Lenin mocked Bauer's inconsistency for 'excluding from his plan for the extra-territorial autonomy of nations the *only* extra-territorial nation'.

These polemics show very clearly that the status of the Jewish diaspora, like the concept of diaspora, are not self-evident notions. The same could be said of any diaspora, for no one can predict whether it will survive as a cultural minority, endowed with more or less autonomy depending on where it is settled, or whether it will disappear, either through assimilation into the surrounding environment, or through the 'return' of its members to their land of origin. At the beginning of the twentieth century, the Jews, who did indeed constitute a 'nationality' in some states, did not have a territory to return to, and despite their numbers, their distinctive cultural characteristics (in the Yiddish-speaking communities) and a common religion, there was no agreement among various historical figures to wager on their survival as a distinct people or their disappearance. Neither the genocide nor the creation of a state were in fact *foreseeable*.

One might have thought that the polemic over the permanence and nature of diasporas would have quietened down after the creation of the state of Israel. But it was not so, for while less than about one-third of the Jews in the world are Israeli citizens, two-thirds remain in the diaspora and, if we leave aside those in the Soviet Union and Syria, they seem to want to stay where they are. There is nothing to suggest that the situation will suddenly change; the polemic has therefore been resumed. Will the dispersed Jewish communities (in the United States, Argentina, France, Great Britain, South Africa and elsewhere) be able to preserve their Jewish identity? Is it the existence of the state of Israel that — overwhelmingly — ensures this identity and enables it to survive? Without the existence of a Jewish nation-state, would it not break up? What do the Jews of the various countries of the diaspora have in common for them to be seen as a single people or as being part of the 'Jewish people'? Some deny that the Jewish people exists. In a well-known booklet, Stalin wrote in response to Bauer that the Jews precisely did not form a nation: '... but what common destiny and national cohesion is there, for instance, between the Georgian, Daghestanian, Russian and American Jews, who are completely separated from one another, inhabit different territories and speak different languages?'

Yet the existence of a Jewish diaspora, whose permanence is indisputable, cannot be denied. The genocide gave it a common destiny which even Stalin could not have predicted. But the diaspora is also marked by shared or similar cultural traits in each community — and it is moreover the very number of these communities that, with the state of Israel, strengthens their cultural or national awareness. The historical depth, the multiplicity and the diversity of geographical settlements, the very diversity of the lived experiences act, paradoxically, as positive factors of identity.

In that, the Jewish diaspora shows analogies with, say, the Armenian diaspora. Among both, part of the group is territorialized, part is not. The territorialized part of the Jews — or the Armenians — perceives the whole of the Jews — or the Armenians — as a people, and gives this perception an ideological expression: the whole people must 'return' to the homeland. But the extra-territorial Jews do not see themselves thus. They produce countless definitions of themselves, from the narrowest to the broadest, to understand what they are. And this very effort — as if it was a matter of overcoming an invisible obstacle to the maintenance of collective identity — becomes a positive factor of this identity.

It can be seen thus that the notion of diaspora is at once both objective and subjective. Its reality is proved in time and tested by time. That is why economic migration does not necessarily create a diaspora. In many cases, in the United States for example, European nationalities have not maintained themselves as distinct groups. For a group that emigrates, while it only rarely displays the will to assimilate into the host society and lose its specificity in it, often breaks all contact with its past and with its original home. And why not, after all? The survival of its culture does not depend on its maintaining its originality, since another group, the territorialized one, looks after this culture. The maintenance of the feeling of belonging and the certainty of identity is, in minority situations, a matter of will, of conscious decision and, one might even say, determination. Certainly, the word diaspora is used today to describe any community that has emigrated whose numbers make it visible in the host community. But in order to know whether it is really a diaspora, time has to pass. We are more or less certain that the Chinese, the Gypsies, the Armenians and the Jews 'live in a diaspora', and will survive there for some time yet. For other emigrant collectivities, things are less certain. Diaspora is thus not a reality or a concept whose use is so obvious. Nor is the permanence of any extra-territorial minority obvious. In short, the word is adventurous, for it applies to a human adventure subject to the fortunes of history and fate.

7

Reflections on Genocide

YVES TERNON

The word genocide names the unnameable; it defines the unthinkable and sets off a crime quite out of the ordinary. It gives the dictionary a flexible word that enables us to suffer the unbearable; 'genocide' makes murders ordinary and freezes horror. It is a handy word that can act as a memorial for the peoples engulfed and pronounce an anathema on nation-states. It is a double-edged word: on one side, there are the victims at home for eternity in the paradise of the righteous; on the other, the philosophical executioners and the terrorist governments, a hybrid word taken from two different tongues to speak two languages, the language of the weak and the language of tyrants, the language of law and the language of arbitrariness.

The term genocide is inherently ambiguous. It does not mean what it is supposed to mean. The use of 'genos' is in itself a contradiction. 'Genos' means race rather than tribe, not people, which is 'ethnos'. This leads to the paradox that the word invented to describe the crime takes on board the ignorance of the criminal, and the jurist gives his blessing to a scientific error which he ought to be denouncing.[1] There is ambiguity too in the fact that murder is a crime against an individual, while the slaughtered race is made up of many individuals. In order to speak of murder, there has to be a body. If the victim is only injured, it is only attempted murder. What name should be given to an attack on a collectivity causing many victims but leaving some survivors? Decimation means defining a percentage: group murder implies the absence of survivors. Obviously, it cannot be a requirement of genocide that the group concerned totally disappear. In the most perfect criminal system, some individuals always manage to escape. For the Nazis, *Judenrein* was an absolute ideal, but they were only able to achieve it in a 'purified' Europe in tiny Estonia.[2] The total murder of a race cannot be achieved; strictly speaking, there can be no genocide since a race cannot be individualized and, much less, exterminated. Even in the wildest racist fantasies, the destruction of dolichocephalic peoples by brachycephalic ones — or black-eyed, dark-skinned men by blue-eyed, light-skinned men — has not been programmed; the cranium measurers and the race spotters only supplied broad guidelines: they could not provide

126

total identification of all those against whom to pronounce a verdict without appeal.

Genocide was created in 1944 when, wishing to describe the extermination of the Jews in Europe, the criminologist Raphael Lemkin looked for a word that would fully encompass the dimensions of what was happening. Later, the lawyers who endorsed the word by giving it a legal content redefined it, ignoring its etymology. This neologism in fact brought together two concepts, one of which referred to the identity of the victim, and the other to the intention of the criminal. The victim is a minority of which a government rids itself through extermination or by reducing it to a tiny fraction. Premeditation of murder and identification of the members of the target group are the necessary conditions of genocide. It is a logical crime, a perfect crime in which the murderer forges his alibi and sets himself up as judge, a crime reversing the normal roles: the victim is deemed guilty and called on to justify himself. It is a crime without risks in which the relations of force are unequal. The murderer has his victim at his disposal. Since he arranges, programmes and supervises every stage of the murder, he accomplishes it coldly and one by one reduces the defences of an opponent whom he only finishes off after mortally wounding him. The murderer is not put off by the dizziness of destruction. The end he pursues is terrible but necessary. His rage has an object and he identifies it. In the concept of genocide, the number of dead is less significant than the prior act of selection: separating those to be destroyed from those to be preserved, destroying a difference with the intention of preserving a unity. Genocide does not have a monopoly of horror. The destruction of the population of a city is not genocide since the inhabitants have not been previously selected. The Japanese of Hiroshima are just like those of Kyoto, the Germans of Dresden just like those of Leipzig. The destruction of Hiroshima and Dresden was designed to terrify, not wipe out, the Japanese or German people.

Genocide is a word for lawyers and moralists, but it upsets the political balance. Since the criminal is always a state and states have no choice but to coexist, and since genocide is the sole offence that absolutely prevents a regime from surviving, politics clash with ethics and the dialectic comes to the aid of the crime. Genocide is unacceptable, therefore it has never occurred — at least it is never called by that name. Lies, distortions, falsifications, any means may be used to reject this act, just as they had been to execute it. Thus the murder of a race becomes by a series of interpretations a camouflaged operation of annihilation of a human group by a state convinced that this suicidal act is the ultimate recourse and the necessary condition of its own survival.

Let the file be handed over to moralists, historians or lawyers, and the arguments open on how to describe what happened. Named genocide, the massacre becomes timeless and enjoys imprescriptibility. The supreme cunning of the crime of genocide consists in committing it under another name, in covering one's tracks to sow doubt in order to end up with a massacre that the international community will simply overlook: thus the brand of infamy is avoided. About the Armenian cases, the Turkish ambassador in France stated recently: 'There was no genocide, there were only events.' This tactlessness in the choice of a term revealed a whole collective subconscious: genocide is a non-event which did not happen because it does not suit history.

History of 'Genocide'

The concepts of genocide and the penal responsibility of states were developed at the same time. The principle of a supranational law had been set out in the nineteenth century by the European powers when they intervened in Ottoman affairs on the occasion of the Greek war of independence, then of the persecution of the Jews of Damascus and Rhodes (1840), the Christians of Lebanon (1861) and the Armenians (especially from 1894 to 1896). In a joint statement signed on 24 May 1915, the three foreign ministers of the Entente who had just been informed of the massacres in the Armenian provinces threatened the Young Turk government that after the war it would be arraigned before a tribunal if it did not put an end to its exactions. On 29 March 1919, the first peace conference set out the responsibility of those who violated the laws and customs of war and the laws of humanity. The principle of an international tribunal competent to discuss these violations was included in the treaty of Sèvres, a document which was never ratified and was annulled in 1923 by the treaty of Lausanne. In 1925, the Romanian lawyer Vespasian Pella noted that the state is 'an active subject of penal law'. As such, it cannot ignore the rules of law that it imposes on individuals and at the same time condemn criminals and commit the very crimes for which it is condemning them. In order to establish this principle, the lawyers endeavoured to prohibit recourse to war as a means of settling international disputes — a verdict that was endorsed by the Briand-Kellogg pact in 1928 — and to prevent the destruction of human groups. In October 1933, at the fifth conference for the unification of international penal law, Professor Raphael Lemkin proposed declaring 'delicitio juris gentium' acts aimed at destroying a racial, religious or social collectivity. He classified such offences under two headings: attacks on the physical or social person of the members of the collectivity — the crime of barbarism — and the destruction of cultural values — the crime of vandalism. He suggested the drafting of an international convention for the punishment of these crimes. The plan for this code of punishment was outlined two years later in Bucharest by Professor Pella. He proposed the creation of an international penal tribunal, responsible for ensuring the protection of the rights of man and the citizen against a pathological deviation of the national state. The League of Nations had the means to establish such a body but it only brought forth a convention on the punishment of international terrorism in 1937.

The lawmaker had thus not yet designated 'the nameless crime' denounced by Winston Churchill in a radio broadcast on 24 August 1941. In 1944, Professor Lemkin published a detailed study on the Axis occupation of the occupied countries.[3] He revealed the inhuman practices of Hitlerite Germany and denounced Hitler's programme of destroying the peoples of occupied Europe, with the aim of Germanizing their territories. In order to characterize the crime, he coined the word genocide:

> By 'genocide', we mean the destruction of a nation or of an ethnic group... Generally speaking, genocide does not necessarily mean the immediate destruction of a nation... It is intended rather to signify a coordinated plan of different actions aiming at the destruction of essential foundations of the life of national groups, with the aim of annihilating the groups themselves. The objectives of such a plan would be disintegration of the political and social institutions, of culture, language, national feelings, religion and the economic existence of national groups, and the destruction of the personal security, liberty, health, dignity, and even the lives of the individuals belonging to such groups. Genocide is directed against the national group as an entity, and the actions involved are directed at individuals, not in their individual capacity, but as members of the national group.[4]

Genocide thus describes an elaborate, complex programme, a coordinated aggression against every feature of a national group to render it vulnerable, annihilate it and impose on the survivors the national pattern of the oppressor. From these premises to its more detailed formulation, the concept of genocide belongs to international penal law. It is a legal concept that defines a crime.

The notion of genocide appears for the first time in an official document on 18 October 1945. The indictment of the Nuremberg Tribunal declared that the accused:

> ... conducted deliberate and systematic genocide, viz., the extermination of racial and national groups, against the civilian populations of certain

occupied territories in order to destroy particular races and classes of people and national, racial, or religious groups, particularly Jews, Poles, and Gypsies and others...[5]

The indictment was enlarged upon in the British address given by Sir Hartley Shawcross:

Genocide was not restricted to extermination of the Jewish people or of the gypsies. It was applied in different forms in Yugoslavia, to the non-German inhabitants of Alsace-Lorraine, to the people of the Low Countries and of Norway. The technique varied from nation to nation, from people to people. The long-term was the same in all cases.[6]

Professor Champetier de Ribes likewise referred to genocide in his case for the prosecution address: 'This is a crime so monstrous, so undreamt of in history throughout the Christian era up to the birth of Hitlerism, that the term "genocide" has had to be coined to define it.'[7]

Yet the word genocide does not appear in the Final Act of 1946. It is to be found in the trials of Nazi war criminals tried by the national tribunals of the Allies, but its use was the subject of a debate among lawyers. Some hesitated to use it: they felt that it was indistinguishable from the formula 'crime against humanity' and was too restrictive in the categories that it envisaged.

The word owes its lightning career to the United Nations Organization which established it permanently in the international legal vocabulary. During its first session, on 11 December 1946, the UN General Assembly adopted a resolution on the prevention and punishment of the crime of genocide:

Genocide is a denial of the right of existence of entire human groups, as homicide is a denial of the right to live of individual human beings; such denial of the right of existence shocks the conscience of mankind, results in great losses to humanity in the form of cultural and other contributions represented by these human groups and is contrary to moral law and to the spirit and aims of the United Nations.

The Assembly mandated the Economic and Social Council to undertake the studies necessary for the preparation of a draft convention. The three experts appointed to give their opinion on this draft were the founding fathers of the concept of genocide: Professors Lemkin, Pella and Donnedieu de Vabres. The concept of genocide thus appeared safe from any deviation. But the representatives of member states intervened in later work.

After moving from draft to report, from committee to commission, after countless consultations and resolutions, the text of the Convention on the Prevention and Punishment of the Crime of Genocide was adopted by the Assembly[8] and submitted for signature and ratification or accession by member states.

Article I
The Contracting Parties confirm that genocide, whether committed in time of peace or in time of war, is a crime under international law which they undertake to prevent and punish.

Article II
In the present Convention, genocide means any of the following acts committed with intent to destroy, in whole or in part, a national, ethnical, racial or religious group, as such:
- (a) Killing members of the group;
- (b) Causing serious bodily or mental harm to members of the group;
- (c) Deliberately inflicting on the group conditions of life calculated to bring about its physical destruction in whole or in part;
- (d) Imposing measures intended to prevent births within the group;
- (e) Forcibly transferring children of the group to another group.

Article III
The following acts shall be punishable:
- (a) Genocide;
- (b) Conspiracy to commit genocide;
- (c) Direct and public incitement to commit genocide;
- (d) Attempt to commit genocide;
- (e) Complicity in genocide.

Article VI
Persons charged with genocide or any other acts enumerated in Article III shall be tried by a competent tribunal of the State in the territory of which the act was committed, or by such international penal tribunal as may have jurisdiction with respect to those Contracting Parties which shall have accepted its jurisdiction.

Intervention by representatives of member states had modified the spirit of the 1946 resolution; the text of the Convention bears the imprint of this intervention. As a global concept, the word genocide met with universal approval. But when it came to putting it into a legal framework, states saw the threat: they were handing over to the UN a legal body empowered to indict them for past, present or future actions. As they could not shirk their duty and refuse to participate in an action designed to strengthen human rights, the representatives of these states took care to draw up a limitative list so as to restrict the document's scope and avoid mentioning in it crimes that their nation might once have committed or that their system might lead them to commit in the future. The only crime on which there was unanimity had been committed by a country that was absent from the debates, whose regime had been finally destroyed, and it was in regard to that regime that the word genocide had been invented. Historically and etymologically, the word genocide was linked to Nazi ideology and theories of racial hatred. This idea, upheld in particular by the Soviet delegation, reduced genocide to an unprecedented historical accident and the purpose of the Convention was to prevent its recurrence.

The UN General Assembly was therefore defining a crime that it imagined it would never have to deal with, and the resulting gap between the initial concept and the text of the Convention is striking. The definitions in articles II and III exclude several offences from the framework of genocide. The word is no longer self-explanatory and requires elaboration to define the victim or specify the method used by the murderer. The only victim groups are national, ethnic, racial or religious groups, seen as constituting identifiable communities. The national group is composed of persons having a common 'national origin'. It concerns not only the citizens of a state or the holders of passports issued by that state, but individuals possessing the culture of that nation, speaking its language and sharing its ways of life, whether or not they remain in that state. The members of the commissions had been unable to agree on the distinction between a national group and a national minority and had avoided pronouncing on this issue. The sub-commission that had to do so charged a rapporteur to propose a definition. He had suggested interpreting the term minority as describing

a group numerically inferior to the rest of the population of a state, in a non-dominant position, whose members — being nationals of the state — possess ethnic, religious or linguistic characteristics differing from those of the rest of the population and show, if only implicitly, a sense of solidarity directed towards preserving their culture, traditions, religion or language.[9]

This distinction does not appear in the final text. An ethnic group is seen as a national sub-group and embraces the racial group. Unable to agree on the meanings of words 'ethnic' and 'racial' while recognizing the irrational factors attaching to the term race and the difficulties of a scientific racial classification, the members of the Commission considered that it was right to maintain the distinction between race and ethnic group: ethnic group referring to biological, cultural and historical characteristics of a group; race applying only, with every possible reservation, to innate physical characteristics. The last group concerned by the Convention, the religious group, comprises 'any community united by a single spiritual ideal'.[10]

The exclusion of political, economic, social or cultural groups limits the scope of the Convention but enables it to exist. The genocide convention is the product of a compromise. Mention of political groups would have reduced the number of signatory states and blocked an agreement on the creation of an international penal tribunal. States refused to grant the UN a right to intervene in their domestic affairs. In return, the Convention tacitly authorized a state to exterminate any group — be it political, economic, social or cultural — not identifiable by its nationality, physical characteristics, ethnic identity or religious beliefs. The UN General Assembly had called for the establishment of a code to protect minorities. The final act, by abstaining from mentioning them, defined groups that were unprotected and indicated to states the categories that they could freely eliminate. It even offered them recourse to verbal hair-splitting by allowing them to move national, ethnic, racial or religious groups into other categories. Whereas the notion of the imprescriptibility of the crime of genocide had not yet been established, faithful to the principle by which no crime or punishment can be defined without a law, the UN sought to legislate to prevent and punish future crimes. By limiting a framework that the determination to safeguard human rights committed it to extending, the Convention as it were redistributed the crime of genocide and simply set out for future states involved new potential means of defence. Among the other definitions proposed subsequently, the broadest reflects the original concept of genocide: 'The crime of genocide in its most serious form is the deliberate destruction of the physical life of individual human beings by reason of their membership of any human collectivity as such.'[11]

The word genocide covers sectarian crimes as well as racist crimes. In the national-socialist nightmare, racism and sectarianism had been mixed up together. The Nazi doctrinaires were convinced both that they belonged to a superior race and that they held the truth. Two propositions were one too many: one would have been enough to destroy any groups that were different. Even when it is only small-scale, genocide has its source in exclusion, whether it is linked to colour, appearance, religious belief or civil status, or to political creed, economic class, linguistic or cultural habits. It characterizes a premeditated crime, aiming at the extinction of a human group defined simply by what it belongs to, and what it belongs to is enough to obscure the individual. National representatives to an international body, called on as politicians to settle matters of ethics, had served the interests of their government and mutilated a concept in order to reduce its practical scope. The Convention only has any meaning if a supranational jurisdiction is in a position to punish a guilty state. Article VI envisages two punishing bodies: a competent tribunal of the state in the territory of which the act was committed, which amounts to proposing that the murderer judge and punish himself; or an international tribunal which has remained a dead letter.

The powerlessness of lawyers handed the word genocide back to historians. Before they will speak of genocide, they see it as essential to study the file, look at the complaint in detail, set out what happened and in what circumstances, examine the sources in order to be able to pronounce definitively on a collective murder, and not to call genocide what was only a massacre, a massacre what was only a security measure or a police gaffe, etc.

Today the word has become widely accepted by public opinion and has been seized upon by the oppressed who at last have available a word to describe what has happened to them or what will inevitably happen to them if this or that state does not stop its persecution. The old victims call for justice and reparations, and the future victims demand the protection of international agencies which, by adopting this rump convention, have deprived themselves of the means of ensuring that protection. Language — and several languages have accepted this word into their vocabulary — is henceforth a prisoner of a term whose meaning is not the same for public opinion, historians or lawyers. This crime, of which it was essential to prevent a repetition, has become a crime that never happened. Common sense, on the other hand, obliges one to recognize that at every period in history genocidal practices have bled peoples and that since the Second World War genocide has occurred with a frequency which endangers the survival of humanity.

Genocides of Yesterday and Today

I have spent ten years studying the genocide of the Armenians by the Young Turks. The case is exemplary but the Armenian people's indictment runs up against the obstinate refusal of the Turkish government which, in order to preserve the heritage of the crime, refuses to accept the reality of it. And yet, after that of the Jews and the Gypsies, it is the least debatable genocide.

It would be pointless to draw up a list of genocides. Like war, genocide is one of the means available to a government to solve political problems, whether the minority is seen as an obstacle to the realization of its goals or is chosen as a scapegoat to divert popular anger. The collectivities deliberately destroyed were so because they opposed the introduction of a new order defined as progress or resulting from a revolution. It is more important to consider the circumstances that lead to genocide than the final act; the list of past genocides only has any interest if it prevents other genocides. Since we have been unable to define the noun, we are obliged to turn to an adjective and to speak of genocidal circumstances, or genocidal massacres, turns of phrase that calm the susceptibilities of the countries incriminated, the adjective seeming less defamatory than the noun.

In the not too distant past, that of the last five centuries, colonialism was the great purveyor of genocides. It uprooted peoples from territories and repopulated them. Whether conqueror or immigrant, the colonist considered the inhabitants of lands he coveted as savages, incapable of assimilating civilization; this justified his conquest or settlement and allowed him, without offending his morality, to treat the natives as he wished. The resort to extermination was usually judged useless and irrational. By eliminating servile labour, the colonist would ruin the colonial economy. The 'pacifiers' used massacres, devastations, population transfers and sought to use terror to hasten enslavement. In this amoral perspective, slavery saved people from genocide. This was, schematically, the case in Africa and Asia.

The discovery of America and Oceania, by contrast, led to the eradication of native cultures. The European was conscious of his superiority and did not consider the natives as beings belonging to the same species as himself. Insidiously, the Enlightenment deprived him of his clear conscience by asking him questions about the inconsistency of his behaviour: is it possible to proclaim oneself the champion of a Christian civilization founded on love and brotherhood and cloak oneself in an ideology advocating the inequality of the races? In Oceania, the European did not ask himself questions about the humanity of the native. The Aboriginals of Australia and Tasmania and the Maoris of New Zealand were simply exterminated: the nature of the territory encouraged genocide. In South America, the conquistadors began by overthrowing the local political systems by executing Indian leaders and reducing the colonized masses in genocidal proportions. This practice lasted for three centuries. From a population estimated at 40 million in 1492, South America fell to 18 million in 1800. The population of Mexico dropped from 25 million to seven million, an even more fantastic fall than that of the most terrible epidemic in history, the Black Death in the fourteenth century. In the Caribbean, the slave society consumed frightening quantities of Indians. In

Cuba, where the losses were estimated at 10 per cent a year, it was necessary at the peak of the bloodiest oppression to renew the labour force every ten years.

It should be noted, however, that most of this fall in population was not due to the deliberate work of the colonists. Unknowingly, they accelerated the destruction of the Indians by importing lethal pathogenic germs to a population with no acquired immunity. The vast epidemics of measles, influenza, typhus or smallpox caused more ravages than the cruelty of the occupiers. Their ignorance of how to use this instrument of population redistribution meant that the colonists depopulated territories that they could have exploited more cheaply with gentler techniques of constraint. Bartolomeo de Las Casas' indictment, considered a model of Christian charity, in fact reflected a better intelligence of colonialism. Instead of treating the Indians like cattle with an estimated production period of between one and four years, it was more efficacious to bring them together in a community where they would preserve their cultural identity and so enable them to produce better and for longer. The Indian population only stood up to servitude in populous and coherent societies. Elsewhere, it was wiped out. Deprived of local labour, Spanish and Portuguese America imported it by carrying off vast numbers from Africa and recruiting volunteers from Europe by kidnap and seizure. Gradually, three servitudes became mixed up together on the South American continent: the Indian, not very resistant, the White which was scarcely more so, and the Black, which succeeded in taking root and surviving despite losses estimated at ten million before 1810. In North America, the immigrants proceeded differently: they first formed a nation on the coast before conquering the interior. No doubt the virtual extermination of the Indians of North America was not wished by the governments in Washington, but it was the inevitable result of a policy of massacres, expropriations, expulsions, deportations and resettlements in concentration camps and the end product of 400 treaties signed up to 1868, none of which was respected.

The only common feature of these four centuries of savage colonialism is the pathological mentality of the civilizer. His king gave him carte blanche. He could dispose as he wished and in good conscience of this anthropoid rabble. Semantic devices are used to suppress these facts so upsetting to the history of civilized Europe; people agree to call these genocides 'ethnocides' and stress the harm done to the culture rather than the suffering imposed on these peoples. The gap between groups and the accumulation of differences — physical, linguistic, religious, cultural and socio-economic — removed moral inhibitions: the crime became meritorious. The victim of genocide had too few similarities to the perpetrator of genocide for the latter to be worried about his right to kill. The racism that underlay these genocides was fuelled more by indifference and contempt than by hatred. By transforming this good conscience into guiltiness, the heralds of the Englightenment obliged the murderers to change their mentality and language. The attribution to all members of the human species of the same rights to life, equality and liberty, and the duty of fraternity, disturbed genocidal habits but did not end their practice.

The Soviet delegates who took part in the preparation of the genocide convention appeared anxious to reduce the concept of genocide to the accident of fascism. Soviet discretion was based on prudence. By accusing Europe and the United States of imperialism, the Soviet Union ran the risk of being criticized for its own imperialism and presenting its interlocutors with the keys of a different analysis of genocide. If racism was the main cause of earlier genocides, doctrinal sectarianism creates the same effects today. Nationalist feeling and political conviction deify the nation or the party and sacrifice whole peoples to it. Genocide is only one of the means justified and necessitated by the end. The exclusion of political groups from article II of the genocide convention made it possible to remove from the list of such crimes the tens of millions of victims of the Stalinist dictatorship. The number of civilian deaths between 1929 and 1954 alone is more than that of all the genocides this century. Mention of colonialism would have been met by mention of totalitarianism and it would have been easy to show that an imperialist state that extends its territory and a national state that colonizes its internal minorities or brings its opponents to heel are using the same criminal methods. Genocide is a gratifying crime. The victim is deprived of his territory, his possessions, his culture, his faith, his identity or his ideology. But whatever the nature of the harm thus done, it is final. The final solution prevents questions being reopened and closes files marked pending. The only alternative to genocide is indeed enslavement since public opinion seems hitherto to have lived with the moral trauma. In the long run, murder is more profitable than enslavement: slaves might one day demand their freedom, the dead cannot. Only colonialism that has eliminated the natives has survived: the land, once cleared of its population, becomes virgin and available for settlement. In the same way national unity demands the sacrifice of minorities, and the triumph of doctrine the elimination of other parties. Whether colonial, national or political, each of these systems proceeds from the same mentality: assertion of the self as absolute truth, rejection of other as different. To limit the concept of genocide to racist crime is to leave nameless murder by nationalist or totalitarian ideology.

Stalin diversified collective massacres by introducing new categories fabricated by the new ideological necessities of the regime he was installing. There, too, it would be easy for the defenders of Soviet communism to sweep these accusations aside. The situations were so varied that unless any attack on a collectivity is called genocide, it is difficult to know which ones can be so called. The question is thus not knowing which of these events were genocides, but precisely stressing the fragility of a concept which would make it possible to prescribe — in both senses of the word: proscription and prescription — monstrous crimes because they cannot be fitted into the list of imprescriptible crimes.

During the four periods of Stalinist terror, collective liquidations manifested the characteristics of a genocide. In 1929 and 1930, between five and 15 million peasants were accused of being kulaks, a doomed label which lumped them in the class of petty bourgeois owners, attributed to them bad tendencies and denounced them as opponents of collectivization. They were expropriated. Several hundreds of thousands were massacred, the others were deported with their families to Siberia. Those who did not die on the way were decimated by cold and hunger in the places to which they were deported.

Forced collectivization led to a fall in agricultural production that the Party had to make up for by requisitions. In the Ukraine, where collectivization had been ill received, the government imposed norms that were too high for the delivery of cereals: famine began in 1932 and lasted until the 1933 harvest. This artificial famine was kept up by a blockade: the Ukrainian republic was isolated; no information emerged from the Ukraine; road blocks prevented starving peasants from reaching the towns. This tragedy occurred in the granary of Europe; the number of victims is estimated at five million.

The 'great purge' of 1936—8 first affected the central bodies of the Party and then reached out over all the republics, hitting all strata of the population. In two years, more communists disappeared than during the Revolution and the civil war: four to five million were arrested, and more than a tenth were executed, an exemplary reduction of a political group by fixing quotas.

In 1943 and 1944 whole peoples of the Soviet Union, accused often baselessly of having collaborated with the Nazis, were rounded up, deported, deprived of their national rights and restricted in their cultural activities. During the summer of 1941, the Germans of the USSR — above all those of the republic of the Volga Germans — along with Greeks, Kurds, Khemchins (Muslim Armenians from Turkish Armenia living along the Black Sea coasts in Adjaria), and Turks were deported as a preventive measure. The 1943 and 1944 operations were carried out most thoroughly.

There were no individual exceptions: membership of a particular national group meant deportation. The depopulation was followed by the installation of settlers, most of them of Russian origin. There were five transfers, executed with extraordinary speed: in November 1943, all the Karachais were deported; between 27 and 30 December, all the Kalmyks were put on goods trains and sent to central Asia and Siberia; on 23 February 1944, a decree of the praesidium of the Supreme Soviet ordered all Chechens and Ingushes to be rounded up, not only in their national territory but in the other Soviet republics, and deported; on 8 March 1944, all the Balkars were loaded into lorries and transferred in cattle wagons to Kazakhstan and Kirghizstan; on 17 and 18 May 1944, the whole Tatar population of the Crimea was deported to Uzbekistan. In total, over a million inhabitants of the northern Caucasus and the Crimea were uprooted. The transfer required the requisition of 40,000 wagons at a time when war was raging and all means of transport were needed for the army. The deportations, true to the tradition of Russian imperialism, may be explained by strategic needs: its unreliable borders threatened the security of the centre. Treason made the purges necessary, hunger in the towns required famine among the peasants, and the incorrigible obstinacy of the kulaks compelled their removal.

Before these four very different events, one hitting an economic class, the second a social category, the third the members of a party and the last national minorities, who would take the responsibility of deciding whether or not it was genocide? Is it so important before one and the same criminal system to stigmatize it here and absolve it there, to recognize that in one circumstance it did not amount to the imprescriptible crime and that in the other it did? Is the death of a kulak more acceptable than that of a Ukrainian, a communist militant, a Tatar or a Chechen? These victims, like those of colonialism, Turkish nationalism or national-socialism were guilty of the same crime: they were different, and this fact threatened a political system. Their annihilation was coldly premeditated and executed. Whether it is a colonial, national, racist or totalitarian perspective, whether it ensures a conquest, achieves national unity, purifies the race or brings about the triumph of the revolution, the crime of genocide is, in the conscience of its author, purified by the holiness of the end.

After the Second World War, collective murder changed appearance. Colonialism became immoral, racism was outlawed, national sovereignty and social revolution were erected into supreme values. The end of colonialism ensured the renewal of genocides. The new nations had a murderous utopia. Yet such violence was foreseeable and inevitable. Colonialism had drawn territorial borders arbitrarily. The great powers had carved up whole continents by drawing lines on maps, disregarding ethnic realities. National independence was offered to plural societies which had difficulty managing relationships among the different groups composing them, differences which had been perpetuated and often fuelled by the colonial empires. How was national unity to be maintained? How were differences of language, traditions, and religion, as well as economic differences among regions and their ethnic groups, to be respected? In the confusion of ethnic groups, one of the groups, usually the largest, always the best armed, would seize power, oppress the minorities and speak in the name of all while serving their own interests. The new masters could often spare themselves a genocide. Elsewhere, the elimination of a minority was a necessary evil. Sometimes — and this was the case of India — powerful drives were suddenly freed: a continent was engulfed in flames and peoples killed one another. But as no one in particular was responsible and there was no deliberate will to destroy, one cannot talk of genocide.

The decolonization of India left 300 million Hindus facing 100 million Muslims. Certainly there was a majority of Hindus in India and a majority of Muslims in Pakistan, but the two peoples were mixed up together and they had to be redistributed. The situation was particularly explosive in the province of Punjab, which had to be divided between India and Pakistan. Before partition, five million Sikhs and Hindus left the Pakistani half and five million Muslims departed from the Indian half. For three months, ten million people, two blocks of hatred moving in opposite directions, passed each other on the roads. A conflagration was inevitable and the exchange was made all the more uncontrollable because the forces charged with escorting the refugees sometimes massacred the columns. Before the partition of August 1947, racial and religious hatred had left between 200,000 and 500,000 victims in the Punjab. The independence of the two states did not calm passions. Pakistan remained a geographical anomaly. The two parts of the country were separated by over 2,000 kilometres: 55 million Pakistanis lived in the west where the central government had its seat, 75 million in the east, most of them Bengalis who felt they were being colonized by West Pakistan. The Bangladesh war of independence broke out in 1971. Between 1,250,000 and 3,000,000 Bengalis were killed, according to estimates; the Hindu population of East Bengal was massacred; non-Bengali ethnic groups, like the Biharis, were decimated. The international commissions of jurists sent by the UN concluded that there was a strong presumption that the crime of genocide had been perpetrated by the Hindus of East Bengal but saw above all in this tragedy the explosion of popular fanaticism, which is not a genocide. The United Nations therefore found it inopportune to intervene.

Decolonization led to the re-emergence of differences that pre-dated the colonial conquest, differences that the colonizing power had taken good care to fan. When, faced with a mosaic of ethnic groups, a federal regime was the only possibility, the competition was particularly ferocious. In Nigeria, which became independent in 1960 and a republic in 1963, the cleavages were at once geographical, religious, economic and ethnic. There were three regions: the north, dominated by the Hausa, Kanuri and Fulani; the west, dominated by the Yoruba; the east, dominated by the Ibo. There were 27 million Muslims, most of them in the north, 20 million Christians, who made up 90 per cent of the population in the east, and 11 million animists were scattered all over the country. The leaders were first Muslim, then Christian, but power was held by the north; it was determined to preserve the unity of the republic. Incidents broke out in June 1966 in the capital; the Muslim population blamed the Ibo. During the five months that followed, above all in Lagos, the Ibo living in the north were massacred. The Ibo then left the north and west of the country and took refuge in the east. General Gowon, head of state of Nigeria, a Christian from the Middle Belt, ordered a blockade of the eastern provinces. On 30 May 1967, General Ojukwu proclaimed the independence of the Eastern Region of Nigeria as the republic of Biafra. The civil war began in July 1967 and lasted two and a half years. Nearly a million Ibo were killed; some were victims of the fighting, others were massacred, most died of famine or disease. International aid in food and equipment failed to enable Biafra to break the blockade by the Nigerian army. Head of State Gowon — and through him the Nigerian state — denied having organized a genocide of the Ibo through famine. After the war, the government tried to integrate the Ibos into the new twelve-state federation of Nigeria. The subsoil of eastern Nigeria contained abundant deposits of petroleum. The Ibo secession and the accusation of genocide made against Nigeria threatened the interests of three major oil companies. Once again, it is putting the question wrongly to ask whether or not there was a genocide. One thing is certain: the Nigerian state was determined to preserve its unity; it would have gone so far as to kill the last Ibo to achieve it. Does the intention of genocide, revealed by the facts, outweigh the debatable reality of genocide, attenuated by the reintegration of the survivors and the partial restoration of their rights?

In Rwanda and Burundi, two new states born of the division of a former Belgian colony, two ethnic communities had always opposed one another: the Tutsi herdsmen and the Hutu farmers. The Tutsi were a minority in Rwanda (14 per cent of the 3.5 million inhabitants). After independence in 1962, they were persecuted. Three years later, in 1965, the Tutsi minority liquidated the Hutu leadership and took power in Rwanda. The Hutu took their revenge a year later in the southern provinces of Burundi where Hutu rebels murdered all the Tutsi they could lay hands on of whatever age or sex. As a reprisal, 100,000 Hutu in Burundi were at once systematically massacred. The Belgian government, the one most concerned by this tragedy occurring in one of its former colonies, spoke of genocide. The United Nations sent representatives to Burundi and, in 1973, the Sub-Commission on Prevention of Discrimination and the Protection of Minorities addressed a complaint against Burundi to the Human Rights Commission. But the Organization of African Unity (OAU) declared its solidarity with President Micombero of Burundi. The OAU did not want to establish a precedent in an Africa torn by ethnic conflicts. In such a case, of which genocide should one speak? The initial one of the Tutsi by the Hutu, which was a popular outburst, or the one organized in reprisal of the Hutu by the Tutsi, ordered by the central government? It is obvious that each of these two groups sought the annihilation of its opponent but the Tutsi held power, had established an apartheid-like regime at the expense of the Hutu and had the means to annihilate them. This case marks the border between genocidal massacre and genocide, a border that is indeed fragile and arbitrary if one thinks of the horrible events that both describe.

In the Sudan, the Arab and Muslim north had always been distinguished from the Christian and animist south. In 1956, Great Britain granted the country its independence and handed over power to the Arab Muslims in the north. The south became their colony. During a rebellion that lasted 17 years, a major part of the population of the south was liquidated (500,000 victims out of three million inhabitants). The southern Sudan finally won a statute of autonomy. Despite its long duration, this genocidal situation was little known to the general public. A few foreign journalists succeeded in reaching the southern Sudan. Their reports revealed the genocide but the observations were fragmentary and the media took little interest in what was happening.

In these three African examples, the ruling ethnic group had available the army and means of economic pressure. Tribal war was also religious conflict and class struggle. The strongest dictated his law and set out the options: enslavement or death. Decolonization reintroduced barbarism with its ancestral methods of extermination. But the moral impulses of the UN had been held back by the political necessities of the OAU. The African organization set as a condition necessary for the survival of Africa the maintenance of the frontiers drawn by decolonization. It feared chain reactions that would reduce the Black continent to a mosaic of ethnic groups. Faced with this risk, local genocides became a lesser evil, a means of cutting one's losses. The fear of partition opened up the right to genocide. Between 1973 and 1978, Idi Amin Dada's soldiers instituted a reign of terror in Uganda and committed crimes of an unspeakable savagery. The Arabs of Zanzibar were massacred in 1964 before the island united with Tanganyika to become Tanzania, and, in Equatorial Guinea, the dictator Macias fell, a victim of his excesses. Accused of genocide, he was tried, condemned to death and executed. This is the only case in which the provision of article VI of the Convention has been applied. In this case the murder was circumscribed, responsibility was put on one accused person, the sentence was pronounced and carried out. The unity of the Congo was preserved by the pitiless repression of attempts to secede and, through its political upheavals, Ethiopia has maintained its rejection of a partition of Eritrea. One has only to dip into the African pond to discover peoples massacred because they are different, victims of the resurgence of hatreds, swept up because they spoke out for their right to self-determination.

In Africa, genocide was imputable to racial hatred rather than sectarian hatred. Two Asian examples illustrate the strength of sectarianism, whether of right or left. In 1964, the Indonesian Communist Party was preparing a *coup d'état*. Out of a population of 120 million, it had ten million members, a quarter of the adult population. Behind the army, the Muslim party represented the class of landlords of central and eastern Java. To forestall the communist *coup d'état*, the Indonesian army — which had lists of members of the party — had them arrested and massacred. The communists were hunted down right into the villages. The massacres were extended to other categories, such as the Chinese merchants of northern Sumatra. The number of victims was estimated at between 200,000 and 500,000. No one spoke of genocide. Emboldened by its impunity, the Indonesian government repeated the offence in 1975 and had soldiers exterminate the inhabitants of the eastern part of Timor, a little genocide of no importance, tucked away by the international community at the back of its mind (100,000 victims).

The methods used by the Khmer Rouge to build a new order plunged the West into a state of amazement and indignation whose only precedent was the revelation of the Nazis' system of concentration and extermination camps. Although strange, the first measure taken on 17 April 1975 had aroused the curiosity of a public opinion that was favourable to those who had defeated the American army. The soldiers from the mountains evacuated a city of 2.5 million inhabitants in a few days. This experiment, unprecedented in history, was deemed interesting, a revenge of the countryside over the towns, of ignorance over knowledge, of the old world over the new, the return to rural life of a people sullied by Western civilization. By getting rid of Phnom Penh, Cambodia resumed its old ways. When, despite the total isolation of Cambodia, information filtered

out, people realized that dangerous madmen had taken control of a
country and were in the process of annihilating it. The republican army
had been liquidated, the soldiers and their families and the intellectuals
eliminated and, with them, anyone who had received an education, a
religion, any technical training; the family unit was disrupted and the
fertility of Cambodian women seriously affected; four-fifths of the population were sent to work in the rice-fields. The Angkar pushed the logic of
totalitarianism to its limits and its reality surpassed the worst nightmares
imagined by Orwell: there were at least a million victims out of a population of eight million. The accusation of genocide was laid before the UN
General Assembly. Shortly after, North Vietnam overthrew the Khmer
Rouge and installed a new government. The relationships of force were
reversed. The Western governments, previously outraged by the crimes of
the Angkar, were obliged to vote to keep the seat of Democratic Kampuchea at the UN. Faced with the most heinous crime in 35 years, the UN in
turn showed itself to be incapable both of giving it a name, genocide, and
of punishing it. The demands of politics blocked its humanitarian vocation
and pressure groups prevented an intervention in the domestic affairs of a
regime that was yet defunct: in order not to endorse North Vietnam's
coup de force, it was necessary to pretend to overlook the criminal behaviour of Pol Pot's government and keep up the fiction of its reality by maintaining its presence within the United Nations. This was a suicidal dialectic
for the UN which revealed its powerlessness to defend human rights even
when the violation was flagrant.

This short list of massacres that amount to genocides makes no claim to
exhaustiveness, still less to decide whether this or that event should be
described as a genocide. In 1979, during the twelfth Congress of Amnesty
International, Seán MacBride, surveying the genocidal massacres that had
occurred over the previous 20 years, mentioned those of Indonesia, Chile,
Kampuchea, East Timor, Uganda, Argentina, Central Africa and Equatorial
Guinea, but omitted those of Bangladesh and Burundi. The word genocide
had been conceived in a spirit of prevention. Excessive use of it ran the
risk of making it ordinary, too restrictive a use of it risked removing its
preventive effect. Modern information techniques are developing along
with the techniques of extermination. Laid on as television spectacles, the
charnel houses are becoming familiar. As Camus used to say, 'The victims
have just entered the extremity of their disgrace: they are becoming
boring.' Faced with the failure of international bodies, at once both judges
and parties, who will decide to formulate the accusation of genocide?
Against the background of two world wars, lawyers had established
barriers to defend civilization and envisaged punishing war crimes. They
had set out the notions of war crime and crime against humanity. The elab-

oration of the concept of genocide was to be the centre-piece of this preventive medicine and the imprescriptibility of genocide achieved in 1968 was to eradicate once and for all humanity's suicidal evil. But it pushed ethics too far into the political arena. For the accused states, the treatment was more mortal than the disease. Genocide remains the crime of others. Having become ineradicable, it has never happened. And, for good measure, the falsifiers are today attempting to suppress the memory of the event that served as the reference point by denying the reality of the gas chambers in Poland.

The World of Genocide

Genocide is a tragedy with three actors: the murderer, the victim and the witness. Each protagonist is a numberless plural and the individual disappears behind a collective identity. The spectacle of the victims is the most obvious. Ruins and ashes, bits of bodies, charnel houses, rivers of blood and crematoria ovens — horror is a very ordinary word to describe the totality of the upheavals that the putting to death of a collectivity represents. The identity of the victim is scarcely more significant. Genocide has become a crime of close relatives, and skin colour no longer designates the victim any more than does appearance or language. As for religion or ideology, they are not visible and one cannot question a corpse to find out what his beliefs were. Wars are not fought in uniform for nothing. The first stage of genocide consists in restoring to the victim his uniform through a process of identification. The individual only appears during this short phase of the process to receive a label before he is sent back to the anonymity of collective murder. The victim is characterized by the fact that he belongs to a group which is usually a numerical minority. It is rare that the minority situation is defined by a relationship of forces, that is that a minority in power exterminates the majority it governs. Not because it never has the intention of doing so or that moral barriers inhibit it, but for a simple, practical reason: the need for the manpower necessary for production. Servile labour and genocide are antagonistic and while a racist government like that of South Africa meets the conditions preliminary to genocide, it will hardly risk resorting to this extremity since its fortune rests on slavery, not on collective murder. Genocide does not belong to the same immoral category as the exploitation of man by man.

The witness, that is public opinion, is external to the tragedy. It has retained the moral values to which it refers to punish genocide. Informing it and moving it remain the last hope of groups condemned to disappear. Public opinion can be manipulated. It hears the complaints of the victim and the justifications of the murderer. The use of the word genocide is a guarantee of outrage. The intensity of the reaction to genocide, the genocide-effect, is controlled by the media. They can keep quiet about genocide or publicize it, make it far away or bring it closer, and, as they wish, inflate or reduce what is happening. Thus the effect is measured: disinformation or silence if what is happening upsets the political game, full reporting if it makes it possible to discredit the adversary.

It is quite obvious the word worries people — and great care has always been taken to avoid defining it in its legal definition — since it designates a collective criminal behaviour. In nature, man is the only creature to destroy members of his own species. An animal is instinctively warned of the suicidal risk of the crime against the species. Through racism, or through religious or doctrinal fanaticism, civilized man has introduced artificial divisions within the species. He has concocted the elements of an obsessive neurosis without guaranteeing himself against paranoid disorders. The hatred of man for man is the primary cause of genocides. A crime of hatred, a family crime, a return to the first murder, that of a brother by his brother. Cain is obsessed by Abel but cannot escape from the necessity of murder. He is incapable of controlling his impulse and mastering his emotions. Murder becomes liberating: there is a substitution of values. The idea prevails over morality, the primacy of the cause removes scruples. The drive for efficiency fuels partisan hatred and pushes it to the most diabolical extremes. Only an ideology that abolishes the moral values created by man can lead one human group to destroy another. It does not matter much whether this ideology is a religious faith, a national passion, a political doctrine, a racist fever or a tribal hatred. The murderer is convinced of the need to destroy the other because his difference is a threat and his elimination is the condition of his own survival. It is an idea that is disordered in its premises but, given these, it unfolds logically. At the heart of the crime is the paradox of the other, the other who is identical, the double who is intolerable, whom the criminal can only eliminate by erasing the similarity and deepening the difference. Murder only becomes bearable if the victim is first deprived of his human condition. Then the law is not broken since the victim is no longer covered by it.

Membership defines guilt. The members of a group are guilty of being what they are and not what they do. The gap is widened between 'them' and 'us'. They are not people like 'you' and 'me', they are not human beings. Language then turns to the semantic universe of zoology and medicine. The metaphors arise as circumstances or events demand, borrowed especially from the bestiary: little rats, baboons, dogs, jackals, hyenas, vipers; or the imagery of disease: syphilis, vermin, bacillary infections, parasites, lice, and above all cancer, with its surgical treatment: the criminal transforms his vision of the world (the *Weltanschauung* of the Nazi ideologues). It is both manichaean and messianic. The imminence of a utopian society strengthens the messianic faith and authorizes any and every form of violence. The radiant future demands the destruction of the other. The absence of alternative is the guarantee of his elimination. To reach this end, the criminal multiplies the antitheses and launches his anathemas: the lamb of God versus the whore of Babylon; the man of faith versus the infidel; the revolutionary versus the reactionary; the proletariat versus the bourgeoisie; the patriot versus the traitor; the people versus the enemies of the people. Once he has adapted his mentality and his language, strong in his God, his people, his nation, his doctrine or his race, the murderer simply has to strike the pariah group. He is cleansing, purifying, removing, exonerating. This gesture ensures his salvation and that of those with him, in this world or the next.

The aberration in the formulation of the prescription does not remove the intellectual functions of the murderer. He remains artful, subtle, hypocritical and attentive to himself. In this plural of the crime, the leaders are separate from those who carry it out. Genocide is a murder at several levels which, always, descends from the top to the base. The hatred of a single man cannot secure the perpetration of a genocide. His delirium is only communicable because it is transmitted and is already shared. Charles IX (or Catherine de Medici) was no more responsible for the St Bartholomew's Day massacre than Alexander III was for the first wave of anti-Semitic pogroms. Hitler, Stalin, Talaat are at the top of the pyramid. They give the order and cause a world out of kilter to tip into the horror. The only guilty party is the idea. The leaders are empowered to arrange it. Compared to those carrying it out, they have the privilege of thinking and organizing genocide: they are the strategists of annihilation. They bear the responsibility for having conceived the crime and set out its methods.

The technique of thorough genocide rests on three successive operations: identification, uprooting, extermination. Selection, discrimination and segregation are synonyms for the same act of separation that aims in an apparently uniform whole at labelling the differences. From marking doors to the yellow star or the roll call, the process is the same: the individual appears briefly before falling back into the group. He receives a dress or a number which marks him out for death. Uprooting is doubtless not necessary for the accomplishment of a genocide, but it facilitates its execution. Removed from its natural milieu, the group becomes more vulnerable. The massacre on the spot is dirty, messy, traumatic for the killer, destructive of property. Deportation has the simplicity of the neutron bomb: it wipes out men and preserves the environment. Regrouping in camps diminishes resistance, facilitates extermination and makes it possible to camouflage it, to give it the appearance of a natural death. Genocide is in fact an easy game in which the victor is designated beforehand, a violence that goes only one way. The risk is not, as in war, a risk that is shared.

Could the nations which, through history, have professed cynicism, advocated the law of the strongest and rained curses on the conquered, forego conquering without risk by carrying out crimes that are so profitable and have such a high return? They could, on condition that they rise to a higher awareness of their actions and admit that ethics challenges the political to erase it without suppressing itself. The memory of the murder pursued Cain. The murderer stands in front of a mirror and contemplates his suicide. Through the collective breach of the taboo, death enters into apotheosis. Terror runs a cycle. Whether it is a matter of a single crime or thousands of crimes, of the crime of a single individual or that of a collectivity, one can only kill on condition that one dies oneself. The first revolutionaries accepted the exchange of lives. They recognized their guilt and demanded their punishment: this was the price paid for the defence of the idea. Then, with the birth of the modern state, came the era of Shigaliev. The revolution cast off morality. Naked, the idea becomes absurd and indecent. When it has recourse to genocide, it is neither treatable or curable: it is convulsed and entering its agony. The robber is robbed. He thought himself subtle, untouchable, unpunishable. Once the murder has been accomplished, the criminal discovers the nothingness of his own death. He is delivered from his obsession: it preserved him. The crime cannot be dissociated from the punishment.

Notes

1. This verbal vagueness is, however, less important than the use of the word holocaust which, while it recalls an event unique in the annals of crime, implies that the victims are offered as a sacrifice to be burned.
2. In fact, some Jews from Estonia managed to reach Sweden.
3. R. Lemkin, *Axis Rule in Occupied Europe*, Washington, Carnegie Endowment for International Peace, 1944.
4. Ibid., p. 79.
5. *Trial of the Major War Criminals before the International Military Tribunal*, Nuremberg, 1947, vol. I, pp. 43–4.
6. Ibid., vol. XIX, p. 497.
7. Ibid., vol. XIX, p. 531.
8. Resolution 260 A III of 9 December 1948.
9. E/CN. 4/Sub. 2/384/Rev. 1, para. 568.
10. E/CN. 4/Sub. 2/416/para. 78, p. 21.
11. Peter N. Drost, *The Crime of State*, Book II, *Genocide*, Leyden, A.W. Sythoff, 1959, p. 125.

Ethnocide and Acculturation

FRANCOISE FONVAL

The term ethnocide has been coined on the model of homicide and genocide. One could push the analogy with homicide further by asking the question: are there two forms of ethnocide, intentional and accidental?

This apparently ironical question goes right to the heart of the debate about genocide: at one extreme, unfortunately common throughout history and down to our own days, ethnocide is conceived as a deliberate policy of destroying a culture which often leads to the physical destruction of the members of the society bearing this culture, that is to genocide. At the other extreme, one finds societies gradually losing their ethnic identity in favour of a different culture, smoothly and without apparent resistance on the part of the population concerned. This process is also often called ethnocide by many social science experts.

All the intermediate processes of assimilation and integration — also designated by the names acculturation, transculturation and deculturation — are almost always defined as ethnocidal. Does this mean that the concept of ethnocide covers an equally wide spectrum of phenomena and processes?

The complexity of the problem is obvious. The ambiguous use of the concept of ethnocide gives ample scope both to the detractors and to the defenders of ethnic or cultural identity to draw diametrically opposed conclusions from identical facts. Thus national integration, which is at the root of most minority situations, is considered as primary in newly independent countries and the ethnic demands unsatisfied by these new nation-states are outlawed because they are accused of dividing the people, of going against its basic interests and of undermining the efforts at nation-building and consolidation. This attitude, particularly apparent in Latin America, has as its counterpart the systematic defence of every minority and every culture whatever its characteristics, age, or size and even whatever the will of the populations concerned.

Can one in any case speak of ethnocide where there is no ethnic group, or no longer one, but where one or other of the constituent characteristics of the latter has been retained, whether it is the language, religion, traditional

territory or any other 'difference'? None of these traits is in itself sufficient
to define an ethnic or cultural minority. What is needed for such a definition, in Shirokoroff's words, is 'a collectivity of awareness and will' of
a human group in relation to one or more other groups. And for there to
be ethnocide, inter-ethnic relations must be established on a domination/
dominated pattern whose logical end-product is the destruction of the
dominated culture or its absorption (integration, assimilation). This
phenomenon has become universal since, as Sélim Abou says,

> ...there is no nation in the world that does not seek to function as a
> super-ethnic group harbouring shared cultural traits capable of counter-
> balancing or even dominating the cultural heritages of the ethnic groups
> that it embraces and arousing among the whole population, however
> heterogeneous it is, the feeling of a common destiny that has a greater
> capacity to mobilize than the particular ethnic origins.[1]

Obviously, the most radical way to attain this objective is the pure and
simple elimination of the 'other' by genocide: millions of people have thus
been massacred all over the world because of the way others considered
them in ethnic terms.

Ethnocide is a slower process. Based initially on ethnocentrism, ethnocide relies on the conviction among members of an ethnic group of the
superiority of their culture in relation to all others and thus the rejection
of otherness. But for there to be genocide, this conviction must be transformed into action, since ethnocide is a conscious policy of destruction of
an ethnic group. It proceeds from a deliberate purpose usually derived
from the economic and political reasons of systems which function according to their own logic of intolerance and are extremely coercive for the
groups they aim to destroy. Ethnocide thus does not encompass the
natural or spontaneous processes of cultural change or acculturation which
are found throughout history all over the world. Yet here an important
nuance should be introduced: in fact, a large number of these so-called
natural or voluntary processes are induced by means that are often hidden
or apparently alien to the processes in question, the most effective of
which are surely today the mass media — television, radio, cinema, press
and others — as well as the new technologies. It is hard to deny, even in
the absence of a will to destroy or, more subtly, to seduce, the formidable
impact of these processes, and their effective ethnocidal power when they
are the instrument of a single ethnic group — or a culture or a society — is
not at all surprising.

In fact the problematic of ethnocide is quite clearly centred on the
power relationships among groups: the strongest — whether or not it is

numerically in the majority — is the one that has political and economic power. It tends more or less systematically to impose its dictate on all the other groups existing within the same frontiers, and sometimes beyond. This phenomenon is accompanied at the present time by a general tendency, at the world level, towards the uniformization and internationalization of a culture, which can be called a 'consumer' culture, which is linked to the internationalization of finance, the media and technology.

At the same time, and doubtless largely in reaction to this phenomenon, we are witnessing everywhere a considerable reactivation, if not a resurgence, of ethnic, regional and particularistic movements, intimately linked to the human need for identification with a group with human dimensions. This demand for a group identity is all the more powerful, dramatic even, when the awareness of belonging to it is acute among the members of the group and when it is at the same time thwarted by the dominant group.

Yet it would be absurd to treat as negligible the power of fascination exercised by the culture (in its broadest sense) of a rich and powerful dominant group. There is often a tendency to confuse — and this confusion is often carefully kept up by the dominant group — access to a degree of material comfort and the practice of the culture of the group or groups already possessing it. Thus the general error arises essentially from the identification which is so often made between the economic and/or social situation of a group and its own identity (poverty, for example, is commonly considered as an attribute of Amerindian cultures, etc). The path is then clear: in order to attain a comfortable situation, or a situation of power, in the national society, the cultural characteristics of the dominant group have to be acquired and those of one's own group lost. This process, which was long considered the only possible one along with the isolation and segregation of the minority group into 'reserves' or 'reservations', has been radically called into question in recent decades by most of the sociologically minority groups in the world. These claim both the right to keep their own identity and the right to choose the material culture and the technologies and the means of communication that suit them. A particular Indian group, for example, may want a radio station to communicate in its native language or may set up a dispensary for the sick without desiring to alter the culture of its ancestors even if the dominant culture seeks to use these same means to impose its own values.

The interplay between traditional culture, material advances and freedom of choice is complex and there are no certain answers. But it is time to stop looking at interrelations and interactions between groups in purely manichaean terms. In so far as the dominated group continues to have some room for manoeuvre, there are no wholly innocent groups facing wholly guilty groups. Instead there are different groups, some of which hold more power than others. This type of situation cannot be evaluated simplistically in terms of inferiority or superiority, absolute guilt or absolute innocence without the risk of losing all or part of the true nature of the problem. A more complex approach is required in which each situation is examined in its specific context. It is only then that it will be possible to know whether the integration of a group involves acculturation or genocide.

Note

1. Sélim Abou, *L'identité culturelle*, Paris, Anthropos, 1981, p. 35.